RECAPTURE
the WONDER

RAVI ZACHARIAS

RECAPTURE
the WONDER

INTEGRITY®
PUBLISHERS
Nashville

Published by Integrity Publishers, a division of Integrity Media, Inc., 5250 Virginia Way, Suite 100, Brentwood, TN 37027.

HELPING PEOPLE WORLDWIDE EXPERIENCE *the* MANIFEST PRESENCE *of* GOD.

Published in association with the literary agency of Wolgemuth and Associates, Inc., Orlando, Florida.

Cover Design: David Uttley
        UDG | Designworks
        www.udgdesignworks.com

Interior: Inside Out Design & Typesetting

Library of Congress Cataloging-in-Publication Data

Zacharias, Ravi K.
Recapture the wonder / by Ravi Zacharias.
    p. cm.
Includes bibliographical references.

ISBN 1-59145-018-7 (hardcover)
ISBN 1-59145-095-0 (international trade paperback)

1. Joy—Religious aspects—Christianity. 2. Christian life. I. Title.
BV4647.J68Z33   2003
248.4—dc21   2003008209

Printed in the United States of America
03 04 05 06 07 RRD 9 8 7 6 5 4 3 2

To Fred David, John Teibe, and Sam Wolgemuth.

These three men introduced me to Jesus Christ, the source of all wonder.

The gratitude in my heart can never be fully expressed in words.

The debt only enriches my heart.

CONTENTS

ACKNOWLEDGMENTS

I WAS SO HONORED when Byron Williamson and Joey Paul from Integrity Publishers first talked to me about writing on this subject. This has been a theme on my heart for many years, but I never felt quite up to it. My original hesitancy was because of the grandeur of the theme and the need to do justice to it. With their sincere encouragement, even to the point of thinking through an outline for me, I felt I would accept the privilege and do my best. My heartfelt thanks to them and to everyone at Integrity. They live up to their name.

As usual, there are two who always help beyond the call of duty. Danielle DuRant, my research assistant, knows where to go for what I need and has now colabored with me for so many years that I would be quite lost without her help. Finally, and always most significantly, my wife, Margie. With quiet confidence she will question that which is not clear and affirm that which really touches her heart. What an invaluable asset she has been. She edits the manuscript and deservedly has the last word.

I would be remiss if I did not thank my colleagues at work again—they ungrudgingly allow me times of absence to get the work done and "cover the bases" for me in my absence. They make my life more wonderful.

None of this, of course, would be smooth sailing without my friend and literary representative, Robert Wolgemuth. He does what he does so well, and I am the receiver of the blessing as a result. His dad is one of those to whom this book is dedicated.

INTRODUCTION

D URING THE THREE DECADES that I have crisscrossed this globe and seen much of the world, I have frequently been asked what my favorite city is or what food I enjoy the most. The latter is easier to answer than the former because, while cities have attractions for different reasons, the palate is conditioned by one's land of birth.

Strangely, I have never been asked for my favorite sight. Now, that is a tough one. I am not sure I could pick a single spectacle, but I know one experience that would be in the running as the most emotionally moving moment for me. One brilliantly sunny day, I was driven from Cape Town to very near land's end in South Africa—Cape Point. As my colleague and I stood there, staring into the wild blue yonder, the sight was utterly breathtaking. Yes, I have seen the Taj Mahal and many of the other so-called wonders of the world. But this was sheer enchantment! Whether it was because we were not expecting such a banquet for the eyes, or whether it was just some preconditioning from a busy day, I would not even venture to analyze. All I know is that the scene affected both of us in the same way.

We stood at the edge of the land and watched as the waters of the calm Atlantic and the restless Indian Oceans collided into one massive torrent of fluid strength, the power of the current almost visible to the naked eye. That body of water has been the graveyard of many a mariner trying to navigate his way around the globe. The endless horizon, the borderless blue and turquoise of the mighty waters, and the frothy white tips of the crashing waves as they collided against each other—this scene from the world's end seemed to overwhelm us with a stupendous sense of awe. For seem-ingly unexplainable reasons, my eyes filled with tears. I was in the throes of enjoying the wonder and the vastness of creation. I felt at once both dwarfed and elevated, dwarfed because my entire stature as a human being seemed so diminished compared to the display of beauty and power before me but elevated because I could revel in this glorious sight while the land and water combined could not exult in its own beauty or share in my delight. Enchantment needs a mind, and the emotions are given as a wellspring.

But then a strange, unexpected sensation took hold of us and we both did something that neither of us had ever done before. We walked back a few steps, found a sharp stone, and scratched the names of our wives onto the surface of a massive piece of rock, real-izing that in a matter of days the writing would be erased. But the thought and act spoke volumes. We had been in the throes of wonder and the moment seemed incomplete without being able to enjoy it with the ones dearest to us.

That awe-filled experience is more than just an illustration to me. It summarizes for me what life is intended to be—the thrill of wonder and the irresistible urge to share it.

That is what this book is about. Each of us has known a moment in which everything in life that is beautiful and overwhelming was suddenly crystallized into a bite-sized moment. Every sense was involved, almost like a convergence of all that is true and good and beautiful, so that we wished we could have frozen the moment and made it last forever. But God, in His infinite wisdom, has shown us that life was never meant to be that way, no more than salt is intended to be eaten by itself or, for that matter, than any seasoning is meant to be enjoyed apart from the food it is enhancing.

How, then, does one retain a sense of wonder without being permanently entranced? How does one live in such a way that the mundane blends with the dramatic so that the whole story remains sensational? How does one take the emotional high points and successfully balance them with the sharp edges of sorrow that are also part of life? How do we live so that we avoid becoming, at the end of life, the proverbial cynic or the "grumpy old person"? Why must that be? Like the wedding at Cana of Galilee, can the best not be saved for the last? It can. It will take the touch of the Master and that is the miracle only He can perform; however, we must fill these jars of clay according to His instructions if the conditions are to be met for celebrating life right to the end.

May these pages help us capture that truth and recapture the wonder. That is the way the Shepherd of our souls intended us to live.

I sincerely hope this book will lead us to the knowledge that befits the title—*Recapture the Wonder.* It could just as easily have been called *Recaptured by Wonder* because, in a sense, it is not as much about something we may possess as it is about what possesses us. Join me on this journey of thought as we savor the delicacies God has prepared for the imagination and the mind, delicacies that time will only enrich.

1

The tragedy with growing up

is not that we lose childishness

in its simplicity,

but that we lose childlikeness

in its sublimity.

CHAPTER ONE

We Miss It, but What Is It?

It HAPPENED AGAIN THE OTHER DAY as we were in one of the teeming cities of our land. My wife and I were walking hurriedly to keep an appointment. We were elbowing our way through the mass of people, bobbing and weaving, a step here and a turn there, making the best speed we could. When waves of humanity descend from every direction, it is inevitable for one to feel like a minute drop in a mighty torrent—unobserved, unimportant, almost non-existent. It is the way with crowds. Such settings at once multiply and diminish the individual.

Yet one man stood out, and we could not help but find our gaze, almost with guilt, riveted upon his stooping figure. Our pace and, yes, our heartbeat, irresistibly slowed. We were both silent as we watched him—unkempt, unwashed, unshaven, and, I suppose, uncaring—as he burrowed through the garbage can on the sidewalk, tearing open any paper bag that might contain remnants of food. This is sobering to see anywhere, yet even more so in a land whose name is synonymous with abundance. But there he was, foraging almost like an animal for any edible morsel and stuffing it into his mouth.

Whenever we see a person whose whole being reveals the marks of such impoverishment my wife remarks, "To think that he was once a baby, held in the arms of his mother while she dreamed great dreams for him." I suppose that only from a mother would these sentiments flow at such a sight. Her words conjure up the image of a mother lovingly cradling her tiny infant and stroking his face while she sings to him about his future. Being human we assume that hopes and dreams are made for us and that we are made for them. In some cultures parents consult astrologers and determine the baby's name according to planetary alignments, and they celebrate with endless ceremonies to ensure a wonderful future. A baby throbbing with life is embodied promise. The birth day gives birth to more than a life—it gives birth to new hopes.

Some analysts of human psychology even go so far as to say that it is this distinctive of the human mind, its grand potential for dreaming and pursuing those dreams, that sets us apart from all other entities. We look into the future not just whimsically but with purpose and design. Our imaginations encourage us to aspire, hope, express ourselves, long for the fulfillment of dreams, wish, and plan. First, others dream for us; then the dream is our own. First, we see circumstances, then opportunities. And so, when we are confronted by a sight such as this pathetic, elderly man searching for sustenance in a garbage heap, we conclude that his life has fallen short of the future he could have had.

Skeptics would use a tragedy like this to point to the absence of God in the human experience. "Where is God in such disfigurement?" they will argue. "How can one blame this man for seeing no purpose and fulfillment in being alive?"

I think it is here that we make our first very subtle mistake, both in our logic and in our experience. It is shallow reasoning to deduce that because pain or unfulfilled dreams have brought disappointment to experience, life itself must be hollow and purposeless. In fact, this conclusion may miss the deeper problem within our common struggle to find something in life of ultimate purpose. Let me change the illustration to make the point.

ATTAINING THE DREAM

An acquaintance of mine was visiting France's famous art gallery, the Louvre. As he was walking silently from room to room, he saw a group of blind students being led by their teacher. Blind students in an art gallery cannot but draw one's curiosity. But the instructor became their eyes, going to great lengths to describe each painting. Then he led them to a room where the statue of an ancient Greek Olympic athlete stood on a pedestal. The teacher took each student's hand, one by one, and guided it so that the student could feel the musclebound figure and the "perfect physique" of this specimen. The young boys were awe-stricken just to touch the powerful body, contoured down to its very veins in stone, all asking if they could feel his muscles once more. Then some of these spindly legged youngsters started to feel each other's thin arms and giggled and chuckled at the difference. Their faces said it all: *What must it be like to have that physique? That's life the way it was meant to be. You have that and you have everything.*

It is here that we grasp the underlying struggle common to both, though in appearance and accomplishment the impoverished old man and the idolized young athlete are worlds apart. No one, for example, would look at the muscular giant and say, "How can there be a God when a man like this looks so good?" No, success and prowess do not logically provoke skepticism about God's existence. But they may lead to an easy delusion—that this well-built champion is a thoroughly fulfilled individual and that life is wonderful for a person so obviously blessed with an enviable physique. Wretchedness and failure understandably breed cynicism. Power and beauty, we assume, bring contentment. One has lost all hope for what he would make of his life; the other has attained the ideal. But the question emerges, Has he really? On the surface it would appear to be true. Yet I have my doubts.

You see, fulfilled dreams are not necessarily fulfilled hopes. Attainment and fulfillment are not the same. Many dream and wish for the attainments that would make them the envy of our world. Careers, positions, possessions, romance . . . these are real goals, pursued by the vast majority who are deluded into believing that succeeding in these areas brings fulfillment. But deep within there is some stronger longing, sometimes even hard to pinpoint. We know there is a vacuum, a space of huge proportions that seeks a state of mind that attainments cannot fill. That dream of ultimate fulfillment is intangible but recognizable, indefinable but felt, verbalized but imprecise, visualized but blurred, inestimable but traded in for something less, something daily. I suggest it is the greatest pursuit of every life, consciously or unconsciously, and it is not mitigated by one's worldly success. That pursuit is the grand theme of this book.

We pity the man at the garbage dump because his impoverishment is stark and his disfigurement is visible. But then we sit in front of our television screens or in movie theaters, or thumb through our fashion magazines eyeing symbols of beauty and success—the icons of our time—and we do not see the scavenging that goes on within them, the searching through every success to find something of transcending worth, the plastic smiles, the contoured shapes, the schizoid hungers for privacy and recognition at the same time. Dreams attained? I think not. They are still looking for "somewhere, over the rainbow."

I believe it is possible that those who have attained every dream may be at least as impoverished as the man at the dump—perhaps even more—as they bask in the accolades, knowing that the charade is shattered by the aloneness within them. We soon realize that the contrast between the two may only be in the access to "things" and in the adulation received, and that it is not necessarily true that in one the greatest hunger—not only to dream, but for the dream to deliver what was hoped for—has been fulfilled. That is the ultimate hope.

What is it that we want the dream to deliver? I would like to call it *wonder,* when life and daily living are possessed and driven by that sense which keeps the emotions in the balance of enchantment with reality. Can life be in tune with reality and also be enchanting without being escapist? It is this very hope that often lies in ruins even though we have attained our personal goals, professionally or economically. All too soon, for so many of us, wonder is swallowed up by wonder-killing reason or experience.

THE PHILOSOPHER'S QUEST

It was Plato who said that all philosophy begins with wonder. Wonder, to Plato, was that impulse that probed, investigated, and sought out explanations. Give a toy to a little boy and in moments it is broken because he has opened it up to see what makes it whir or tick or chime or speak. It is our hidden Narnia into which we long to step and explore. It is the rotating musical merry-go-round that entrances the child. It is the sight of a jet plane or a rocket surging into the skies and the marvel, if only for a moment, at such design and power and beauty. The touch of a hand that makes you wish that time would stand still, the musical score that grips the soul—what makes these things affect us as they do? And perhaps more to the point, why are we fascinated by such things?

MOST OF US CAN GO BACK TO A TIME

IN OUR LIVES WHEN DREAMS

OF A LIFE FILLED WITH WONDER

THROBBED WITHIN OUR SOULS.

Ah! But here comes the rub. This is where we abruptly hit the ground as we touch down upon the mundane. Francis Bacon ruefully observed that though it may be true that all philosophy begins with wonder, it is also true that wonder dies with knowledge. Explanation is the termination point of mystery, analysis the death knell of curiosity. The parts are greater than the whole when you are in pursuit, but they become lesser than the whole when it is no longer a mystery and the toy no longer enchants. In other words, knowing overrides dreaming. Reality undercuts fantasy. Longing often dies at the moment of realization. Is it because description, by nature, defies mystery? Or is it because the reality defies the way we want it to be?

Most of us can go back to a time in our lives when dreams of a life filled with wonder throbbed within our souls. In fact, that very stage of dreaming finds its own fulfillment in a marvelous disposition we call *hope*. But time has led us also to believe that Bacon does have a point. Is it not because of the delight of anticipation that all children love Christmas Eve even more than they love Christmas Day? Is it not because the fulfillment of his longings is just moments away that a youngster, though thoroughly fatigued, will deny sleep and fight to keep his eyes open? But then comes the day after Christmas and reality strikes. The longing is now gone and everything that spelled wonder is being packed up in a box. Does unwrapping the gift take away from the gift? Why is the exhausting pursuit of the human heart for contentment so convoluted? Why does the enchantment that we long for seem so elusive and almost scandalously complex?

Someone once humorously quipped that life consists of four

stages. In the first stage we believe in Santa Claus. At the second stage we no longer believe in Santa Claus. The third stage is when we find out that we *are* Santa Claus. The fourth and final stage has arrived when we *look* like Santa Claus.

We know that hopes come and go and that life returns to the common and the repetitive. If that fluctuation and disappointment were only momentary, we could endure it. But life is not what we thought it would be. The problem with life, then, is not that a man ends up burrowing through garbage looking for something to fill his stomach but that no matter what we have achieved or attained in our life, we still find ourselves burrowing deep within, trying to assuage the hungers of our soul. G. K. Chesterton summed this up when he said that weariness does not come from being weary of pain but from being weary of pleasure.

REALIZING THE FIRST DISAPPOINTMENTS

Something troubling emerges from this realization that greater learning diminishes wonder, that the greater the knowledge the more certain the absence of any transcending wonder. Is the conclusion that life is not enchanting the reason that aesthetic arguments for God's existence are not taken seriously by atheistic philosophers? Denying the objective existence of beauty and design takes away the necessity of explaining the source of my attraction to beauty and the search for a designer, does it not? Why, then, do I feel dissatisfied or cheated and what is it that I am pursuing?

Philosophers who deny this objective reality trivialize the internal longing. That is why we instinctively dismiss their castigations and

PHILOSOPHERS QUESTION THE DREAM

THAT LIFE MUST EXPERIENCE ENCHANTMENT

WHILE ROMANTICS

DREAM AWAY THE QUESTION.

bend our ears to artists, thinking they can help us restore the romance of life. Are they not the ones who perpetually dream? But here, too, disappointment looms, as often these poets and dreamers are more prone to run into pessimism than delight. Everything romanticized seems anticlimactic as one faces the advancing years.

I think of the popular song sung decades ago where a mother's response to her child's question about her future is "Que sera, sera . . . whatever will be, will be." Each time the questions of life are asked, of teachers, friends, and others, the same response is given: "Que sera, sera." Fatalism is on every side, from every source. Finally, the questioner finds herself being asked the same questions and the predictable answer comes: "Whatever will be, will be."

As I am writing this I am aboard a plane heading overseas. The flight attendant, quite intrigued by the fact that I have skipped a meal in order to continue writing, leaned over and asked, "What are you writing about with such intensity?" As we talked, I noticed an engagement ring on her finger and asked if she were indeed engaged. She proceeded to tell me that although she was engaged, she was having second thoughts about it because an astrologer had told her that this was not an auspicious time as he could not see their names aligned in the present astrological chart.

"What do you think?" she asked.

It was hard to keep from shaking my head in disbelief. Where does one begin to talk to someone who is afraid of destiny yet believes in the world of destiny without knowing anything about who controls that destiny? To add to the senselessness of her predicament, she herself did not eat because this was the holy month of fasting. "Que sera, sera" would fit well into her thinking. A million questions surface when one faces the unknown with the grim belief in a predestined life that is at the mercy of who knows what, and that only a sharp, implacable force is in control of one's destiny.

In short, philosophers question the dream that life must experience enchantment while romantics dream away the question. Both disassemble the toy only to discover that the search is greater than the discovery and that they are destined to be resigned to the belief that enchantment is merely a subject to discuss, never a state to be attained. Thus, the arts play with our emotions and philosophy toys with our reason, while every fiber within our being cries out that this is not the way it was intended and that we may have robbed ourselves of the greatest of all treasures. Fatalism is the creed of a will that is dying to its possibilities and seeks to drag the imagination with it. Resignation to life as a "so it is" carved in stone is the cynical response of the one who does not know the grand triumph of the imagination that God has fashioned for us. Just like the bumblebee that flies though it is not aerodynamically fit, so it is that every person who remembers what it is like to be a child gives reason and emotion its due and still seeks for wonder. The flashes in time where we catch a glimpse of wonder spur us on to attaining it.

We have all known that sensation and, like a chord of music that touches the soul, we are possessed by that memory of fullness that transcends words and then with equal mystery is gone. The songwriter captured it well:

> Seated one day at the organ
> I was weary and ill at ease,
> And my fingers wandered idly
> Over the noisy keys.
> I know not what I was playing
> Or what I was dreaming then,
> But I struck one chord of music
> Like the sound of a great "Amen."
>
> It flooded the crimson twilight
> Like the close of an angel's psalm,
> And it lay on my fevered spirit
> Like the touch of infinite calm.
> It quieted pain and sorrow
> Like love overcoming strife,
> It seemed the harmonious echo
> Of our discordant life.
>
> It linked all perplexed meanings
> Into one perfect peace,

And it trembled away into silence
As if it were loathe to cease.
I have sought but I seek it vainly—
That one lost chord divine—
That came from the soul of the organ
And entered into mine.

It may be that death's bright angel
Will speak in that chord again,
It may be that only in heaven
I shall hear that grand "Amen."[1]

Wonder was in that lost chord. There was a "soulishness" to it. It came and then vanished, leaving a hunger behind. How does one describe such an experience? How does one hold on to it?

I strongly suspect that the reason you are reading this book is that you yourself are hoping to find something new and asking whether anyone can deliver on this question. I sincerely believe God has answered, and He has done so in various ways. I have no doubt whatsoever that finding an answer to this question is worth giving everything a person owns. In this answer lies the wealth of our purpose and destiny.

In fact Jesus talks of such a person. He speaks of a merchant looking for a precious pearl who, when he found the pearl of great price, sold all he had previously considered worthwhile in order to buy it. That pearl of great price, pragmatically speaking, is that search for the heart to find its complete fulfillment.

I remember listening to a veteran from one of the recent wars. In the thick of battle, a platoon had lost one of its men and the rest

---

DEEP WITHIN EVERY HUMAN HEART

THROBS THE UNDYING HOPE

THAT SOMEBODY OR SOMETHING WILL BRING

A WAY TO RETAIN THE WONDER.

---

of them wanted to rescue him, even though they knew his wounds were quite possibly fatal. The debate began among the men—should they or shouldn't they risk their lives in what was possibly a hopeless mission? Even the senior officer cautioned that the risk was not worth the returns. At last, two of the men braved the reality and put themselves right in the path of ultimate danger. Dodging the firepower and crawling on their stomachs, they finally reached the side of their wounded comrade behind enemy lines. As he collapsed in their arms, he sighed, "I knew you'd come."

Deep within every human heart throbs the undying hope that somebody or something will bring both an explanation of what life is all about and a way to retain the wonder. Yet if we would but pause and first ponder what it is that we already see in this world of wonder we might get a brief taste of the wonder that may be poured into us as well.

WONDER ALL AROUND

Before I even define the term, let me just lift our thoughts beyond ourselves to the wonder all around us. This alone gives us a hint of how God can carry us to His wonderful purposes in discovering the treasure that is within.

Chet Raymo is professor of physics and astronomy at Stonehill College in Massachusetts. He is a convinced naturalist with a strong mystical bent. Few writers in our time are able to open up vistas of grandeur in the world of objects and entities as he does. In his book *Skeptics and True Believers: The Exhilarating Connection between Science and Religion,* he illustrates in his brilliant and inimitable style the marvels that are all around us in this universe. As a naturalist, he of course doesn't see the need for God in order for him to fully appreciate the wonder he sees, and therefore I believe his position is philosophically weak, though he makes a valiant attempt at probing great themes. That notwithstanding, Raymo is a gifted writer with enormous capacity to describe nature's "wonders," so often ignored or taken for granted by most of us.

For example, he presents in enthralling detail the migratory habits of the species of bird called the red knot. The red knot is a sandpiper that each year journeys from the southern tip of South America to the eastern shores of the United States and beyond and then back again. That round-trip expedition, which covers more than eighteen thousand miles every year, takes the red knot through the arctic islands of the Canadian North, making brief "refueling" stops on the beaches of Delaware Bay and Cape Cod.

The birds begin their northward journey in February each year, hundreds of thousands of them, up the coast of Argentina, over Brazil, with periodic stops to feed. From the northern coasts of South America, they take to the air for a nonstop week of soaring above the Atlantic that brings them around mid-May to touch ground on the marshy shore of Delaware Bay at the very time horseshoe crabs are laying their eggs by the millions. When you consider that during their sojourn in Delaware each red knot might consume 135,000 horseshoe crab eggs, you know they need that stop and time it perfectly. Plumped up for the remainder of their marathon across the vast Canadian terrain, they make their final stop north of Hudson Bay. There, in ideal northern summer conditions, they mate and breed, each female laying four speckled eggs, which she and her mate take turns incubating.

Baby red knots build up their bodies soon with the feathers growing fairly rapidly. There is an incredibly scripted schedule for everything in the process. By mid-July, the females leave the males and their offspring, and start heading south again. The males leave almost exactly one week later. The little ones fend for themselves and then, in late August, they commence their nine-thousand-mile journey to Tierra del Fuego. They begin that flight, their first of such magnitude, without parental companionship. Somehow, with a precise "destination" in mind, as if equipped by flawless radar and instruction, they make their way from northern Canada along the eastern American coast and across the Atlantic to Guyana, Surinam, knowing precisely where to make their sojourns for food. And then, in what appears like a dated and timed appointment, "coming in on a beam," they rejoin the family at Tierra del Fuego for the southern summer.

Here, on the balmy beaches of Tierra del Fuego at the southern tip of South America, they feast, fattening themselves. A long molt and ideal temperatures combine to replace their beaten-up feathers so that they are ready for the long journey back north. What it takes a whole crew of highly skilled men and women at a pit stop in the Indianapolis 500 or a coterie of mechanics and ground staff to get a plane ready for its return flight, the red knot does by its own wit and understanding of natural resources.

Scientists marvel at such genius in the tiny head of a red knot. I might add that the next time we say, "That's for the birds," we had better think twice. Much happens even in their world to remind us of a world steeped in wonder. How does this happen, one might ask? For Chet Raymo, it is just nature's bequest to the red knot. One marvels at such credulity for it defies every basic principle of reasoning in an intelligible universe.

President Theodore Roosevelt had a routine habit, almost a ritual. Every now and then, along with the naturalist William Beebe, he would step outside at dark, look into the night sky, find the faint spot of light at the lower left-hand corner of Pegasus, and one of them would recite: "That is the Spiral Galaxy of Andromeda. It is as large as our Milky Way. It is one of a hundred million galaxies. It is seven hundred and fifty thousand light years away. It consists of one hundred billion suns, each larger than our own sun." There would be a pause and then Roosevelt would grin and say, "Now I think we feel small enough! Let's go to bed."[2]

Is this not the point of the psalmist when he utters, "O LORD, our Lord, how majestic is your name in all the earth! You have set your glory above the heavens. . . . When I consider your heavens, the work of your fingers . . . , what is man that you are mindful of

him. . . ? . . . You made him ruler over the works of your hands"
(Psalm 8:1, 3–4, 6).

When I ponder the wonder that is around us and see the vastness
of its splendor, I also remember what the poet John Donne said:
"There is nothing that God hath established in the constant course
of Nature, and which therefore is done everyday, but would seem a
miracle, and exercise our admiration, if it were done but once."[3]
Donne is making the same point that God made in the Book of Job,
when He asks Job if he knows the mystery of how a bird homes in
on its flight. It is what Jesus was saying in Matthew 6:26, 28, 30:
"Look at the birds of the air; they do not sow or reap or store away
in barns, and yet your heavenly Father feeds them. Are you not
much more valuable than they? . . . See how the lilies of the field
grow. . . . If that is how God clothes the grass of the field . . . , will he
not much more clothe you?" Will not this God of wonder, who has
arrayed the creatures of this world with such inspiring traits, fill us
with His own inspiration? That, I believe, is at the heart of what this
search is all about.

But one might well ask, How do we adequately define wonder?

THE PHILOSOPHERS WHO SOWED THE SEEDS

As I stated earlier, Plato believed that all philosophy began with
wonder until it was replaced by knowledge. He argued that there was
a world of difference between belief and knowledge. Belief, he said,
was the position of a child; knowledge was that of an adult. Actually,
going back to the Greeks gives us a fascinating word and philosophical journey, which perhaps gives us Plato's context. The Greek word

for wonder is *thaumas.* Thaumas was one of the sea gods and his name was derived from the Greek word *thaumatos,* meaning "a miracle or wonder." Thus, by his name he represented all the sea-born wonders.

The world of fantasy and of the fantastic was captured in that word. But this is where it becomes very intriguing. In his *Republic,* Plato relates a conversation between his brother Glaucon and Socrates. Socrates is explaining to Glaucon that human understanding of ultimate reality is more like seeing the shadows than it is grasping the substance. To illustrate his point he imagines a cave in which he sees human beings, chained from childhood, facing a wall with their backs to the opening of the cave. The light coming into the cave from the outside casts shadows of all that is happening on the outside onto the walls of the cave. There is no way, says Socrates, that anyone looking at the wall would be able to distinguish what is real from what is not. They would only know the shadows. If they could be freed and released from the cave, at first the light would blind them, so much so that the most painful thing would be to see the source of the light itself. But over time, they would get used to it and see reality as it really is, including the light itself.

Now, let's pull this all together. Thaumas's wife was Elektra, "the amber-tinged clouds." His daughters were Harpyiai, "the whirlwind," and Iris, "the rainbow." All of these words combine mystery and power, but three in particular have carried over into the English and open a marvelous vista for the eyes and mind.

From "Glaucon," we, in English, get the word *glaucoma,* the disease of the eye that puts such pressure on the eyeball that it puts shadows on everything, resulting in clouded vision. Even in our day, Glaucon is the name of the medication used to fight glaucoma.

"Iris" is that part of the eye that is so beautifully colored itself, with its radial and concentric muscles and contractile capacity to respond to the intensity of light. Through its central aperture, light is processed so that we see the grand tapestry of colors so magnificently present in this world.

And "Thaumas"? I cannot help but wonder if it might be the root word from which we get the Anglo-Saxon name Thomas. It was the apostle Thomas who wondered whether Jesus had really conquered death. It was Thomas who said to Jesus, "I will not believe until I can 'see' and 'touch'" (see John 20:25). And when he saw and touched the Lord, the encounter completely redefined reality for him, which had to that point been prejudiced against the miracle. When he saw the risen Christ, who had delivered exactly what He had promised him—that He was the Way, the Truth, and the Life—his heart was filled with wonder and he knelt in awe, saying, "My Lord and my God!" (John 20:28).

Can it not be our hope as well that the shadows and beliefs of childlikeness become only greater and more wonderful when dispelled by knowledge? Can there not be a reality where the mere world of fantasy is superceded by the fantastically true? Can the rainbow not be the wonderful reminder that we can see beyond the storms? Can the cataracts of matter not be removed so that God's light can reveal the truly spiritual?

After all, what really is wonder?

First, what it is not. Wonder is not merely the same as happiness. Thomas Carlyle wrote in *Sartor Resartus,* "There is in man a higher than the love of happiness; he can do without happiness, and instead thereof find blessedness."[4] Carlyle was on the right track. The

WONDER IS

THAT POSSESSION OF THE MIND THAT

ENCHANTS THE EMOTIONS WHILE NEVER

SURRENDERING REASON.

Spanish mystic Miguelde Unamuno ends his book *The Tragic Sense of Life* with this prayer: "May God deny you peace and give you glory."[5]

Blessedness ... Glory ...

Wonder is that possession of the mind that enchants the emotions while never surrendering reason. It is a grasp on reality that does not need constant high points in order to be maintained, nor is it made vulnerable by the low points of life's struggle. It sees in the ordinary the extraordinary, and it finds in the extraordinary the reaffirmations for what it already knows. Wonder clasps the soul (the spiritual) and is felt in the body (the material). Wonder interprets life through the eyes of eternity while enjoying the moment, but never lets the momentary vision exhaust the eternal. Wonder makes life's enchantment real and knows when and where enchantment must lie. Wonder knows how to read the shadows because it knows the nature of light. Wonder knows that while you cannot look at the light you cannot look at anything else without it. It is not exhausted by childhood but finds its key there. It is a journey like a walk through the woods, over the usual obstacles and around the common distractions, while the voice of direction leads, saying, "This is the way, walk ye in it" (Isaiah 30:21 KJV). It is not at all surprising that of the seventy usages of the word *wonder* in the Old Testament, nearly half of them are by David, the sweet singer of Israel. Wonder and music go hand in hand. Wonder cannot help but sing. Even nature recognizes that.

There is a story I have told before that I would like to tell again here, because there is a marvelous sequel to it. The people I mention are true heroes. They make our world a better place and show the world what wonder is all about, blending reality with a sacred imagination. They live in Connecticut, and several years ago they read of a little boy in Romania who was born without arms, not even an appendage on either shoulder. When he was about one year old they visited the orphanage where he was being cared for because his parents were unable to, and their hearts went out to him. Most of the caregivers in that orphanage would have no more than minimal contact with him because they feared the "evil eye" represented by his deformity and the bad luck they believed he would bring them.

Through discussion and contacts, this couple asked if they could adopt this little one. The boy's mother, as well as many others, questioned the motives of anyone who would take him into their lives and spend themselves in this way, caring for one in such need of nurture and assistance. She asked, "Are you taking him to America so you can use him for experiments? I have heard that they do that in America." Mike and Sharon assured her that this was not their intent at all. They just wanted to give him a home and a chance at life.

"But why would you want a baby like mine?" the mother asked. Sharon had had the foresight to bring a Romanian Bible with her, and opening it to Psalm 139, she gave it to the Romanian mother to read for herself:

> For you created my inmost being;
> you knit me together in my mother's womb.
> I praise you for I am fearfully and wonderfully made;
> your works are wonderful,
> I know that full well.
> My frame was not hidden from you
> when I was made in the secret place.
>
> —PSALM 139:13–15

As the mother read from God's Word, tears started to stream down her face. Finally she looked at Sharon and said, "If this is what you believe about my son, you can have him as yours."

Sharon and Mike brought him back home, where they have loved him and raised him. He learned to use his feet to hold his spoon and feed himself. In every restaurant he and they became the topic of conversation as people marveled at the gift given to him in these parents, the fascinating skill in his feet, but most of all, at his lovable face and sweet personality.

Here is the sequel. Young George is now eight years old. Sharon decided to have a caring Christian teacher train him in playing a classical instrument. You can imagine the hard work and the patience demanded by parents and teacher in such a venture. Naturally, he had to learn to play it with his feet. Some time ago came the first recital and they wondered whether to put him on the program with all the other students. The teacher said she would want him in the program and she would sit next to him as he played. May I just quote the words the father sent to me in a letter? I wept when I read it and I suspect you will, too.

The big night came, and George was nervous and telling us he wasn't so sure if he wanted to do this . . . to make matters worse, there was a much bigger crowd of people than normal for one of these events . . . many of whom had never seen George or met George before. Several students went up to the front and played their various pieces, and very soon it was time. . . . George's name was called. You could have heard a pin drop as the teacher walked up with him, carrying his instrument, a chair and a large pillow that she placed on the floor to lift up the neck of cello. She arranged everything as he needed and nodded for him to go ahead.

There was a feeling of wonder and tension in the room, and at this point my only thought was, "Please Lord, let him just get through this . . ." George began, and the very first note he struck was as sour as could be! He stopped playing, got red in the face, shrugged his shoulders, broke into a huge grin and looked up at the teacher. She warmly smiled back and nodded to him that he should try again.

Well, George then proceeded to play the entire song without a flaw, and it sounded marvelous. When he finished, there was a moment of quiet, and then one of the older students (who is the most advanced student in the group) simply stood in his place and began to clap. Many others in the audience stood to their feet and the applause went on for a very long time. . . . My wife turned to me and said, "George has never once, before tonight, made it through that song without many mistakes!"

Then Mike added these words: "What a great picture of our relationship with our heavenly Father! We are weak, nervous, afraid and flawed and yet Christ stands beside us and warmly says, 'And surely I am with you always to the very end of the age.' God does not hear our sour notes but only the unflawed music and perfection of His perfect Son."[6]

This, may I suggest, is the picture of wonder from every side. The sacred imagination of a young couple, which is greater than the glory of the stars, I might add; the power to inspire a weak young life, not merely to fly on a wing but to play music without any arms; the heartfelt commitment of a teacher who brought music into his heart not merely as a means to cope with life but to celebrate life; the applause of those who recognized what had been accomplished, not merely to be happy for him but to be awe-stricken; the tears of gratitude at the smile of a little life that gloried in the affirmation of those who loved him and gave him this gift. I have to wonder what his biological mother would have said had she been there. Psalm 139 would have now not just been read but heard and seen as well.

There is a postscript. This young family has now adopted a young lad from India with the same handicap. George now has a brother, just as unique as he is but from a different part of the world. The wonder expands.

There is wonder all around us, and it is God's will to fill us with that wonder that makes life enchanting and sacred. We cannot help but sing when that happens. Maybe that is why, of all the religions in the world, there is none with the wealth of music that the Christian faith offers. We sing because His name is "Wonderful." But how do we find this wonder, not merely in His name but in such a way that our heart rests in that delight? We hope the answer is not as elusive as the world has made it to be.

2

Our society is walking through

a maze of cultural land mines

and the heaviest price is exacted as we

send our children on ahead.

CHAPTER TWO

The Rules of the Game

I HAVE JUST RETURNED from a trip to the land of my birth, where I spoke at an event to honor a colleague who was stepping down from his position of leadership to give way to a younger man. It was an emotionally tough day for my colleague and his wife. As one employee after another reminisced, there was humor and recall, all adding to a trip down memory lane. But suddenly something happened. Spontaneously, they all joined in one of the beautiful songs he had written when he was beginning his ministry that spoke of his love for God and his yearning to serve Him. It has a haunting melody and only those who speak the language could truly grasp the sentimental strength of the words that revealed a deep hunger for the heart of God. As the song broke out from the group, within its first strains I caught a glimpse of his wife, a very quiet and lovely woman, who had sat composed all along, now finding herself unable to restrain her tears. The wellspring burst open and the music carried her back to years gone by. None of us could contain the feeling that a tender point was reached. This was a fork in the road and the nostalgia of turning away from the known road to travel a new, unfamiliar way was just too much to handle.

Nostalgia is a powerful tug at the human heart, but within that grip is the recognition of reality. Wonder is a strange and elusive state of mind. We know it when we have it. We talk about it as if we all know what we mean. We wish we could hold on to it forever. Yet we have consigned nostalgia to the days of childhood and fairy tales. The world then was one to be conquered. We were going to soar to heights and breathe new air. The future was like a banquet table laden before us, and we were going to taste its delights to our fill. But now that the years have gone by there is a different emotion. Fatigue, care, worry, mistakes recognized, and yes, even farewells now evict the marvel of what we once envisioned. At best we are sorry that the life invested did not bring the dividends of a compounding fulfillment. This casually penned poem captures the sentiment:

> It's odd God.
> Time's shoeless feet
> sneaked up on me
> and caught me by surprise.
>
> The days of youth I knew so well
> are gone with the blink of an eye.

Innocent play and laughter,
tire swings and fun,
those days were too soon ended
when I thought they'd only begun.

Backyard friends were many
Worries and fears were few.
Hopes and dreams were not yet dashed.
But life as it was then is through.
No longer tree swings,
now they're blowouts
that complicate schedules and work
as I recklessly race down the freeway
in search of a paycheck and perks.

How I long for the years of my childhood,
when life was uncluttered and free.
Perhaps there's a way to reprogram my goals
and capture the me that was me.[1]

I must confess as I read these expressions that I, too, have often felt those very sentiments. But even as I delight in some of those fond memories and echo them, there are twin reactions that somehow nudge their way into my thinking. The first comes more in question form than as an affirmation or counter. "Worries and fears were few," we sigh. Really? Is that true? Or is it now the benefit of hindsight? Could it be that the worries and fears we now have make the ones of younger years seem small, even trite? By the same measure, will the worries of today pale into insignificance ten years from now? Is this just another version of the illusion of "the good old days," making the past seem better than it really was?

Were there not fears then as well? Fears of being rejected, even as a child? Were there not jealousies and envies that burned within our heart? Were there not tears at seeing loved ones being ill-treated by others? Were there not terrors of the night, worrying on some long nights that the morning would never come? Were there not heated words that struck horror into our hearts? How about the fears of not seeing a parent again? I doubt our touchup of the pictures from years gone by changes the reality of the lacerations upon our tender hearts. As children, our lives may have been judged to be worry-free by the adults who controlled them, but even to the young, problems are still life-size. None of this changes the fondness with which we look back at what used to be, but the reality of childhood's struggles certainly merit candor. What, then, is the difference between then and now?

The poet's next line is far more to the point, and this loss we may completely echo in our own heart: "Hopes and dreams were not yet dashed." That, I believe, is what this struggle is all about. What is it that, as children, we hope and dream about that makes life so full of legitimate fantasy? Finding the starting point is not as easy as it may appear.

THE NEED FOR RULES

When I was growing up in India, one of the things we had to learn if we were to play any sport was to be very resourceful. But often our ingenuities had precious little genius to them. I well remember one week of arduous labor as a younger teen when I desperately wanted to play tennis. My buddies and I would watch players from a distance and long to be in their shoes. So we decided we would construct a tennis court in the community park behind our houses. That is the way neighborhoods were built—always with an area for young people in any subdivision to play. I suppose it beat wandering in the malls, especially as there were no such things as malls, anyway.

We walked over to a court at the nearby tennis club and, in crude fashion, measured the markings of the court by our strides. Within a couple of days we had iron posts dug in and positioned to anchor the net. We then ground some limestone and, using a string to measure, marked the boundaries of the court with the powdered stone. Finally, we got a few old bedsheets from our moms, sewed them together, and made sure that the cumbersome fabric would extend over the width of the court. It took some real tugging and elbow grease. We were all set to play our first game on this bumpy, makeshift, stone-littered tennis court, the work of labor and love for the game.

All day at school, I anticipated the first match. I visualized belting a forehand across the court to leave my opponent flat-footed. The moment arrived and we installed the "net." Friends watched when two of us took to opposite sides of the court. As we got ready to serve, we discovered a "minor" problem. We could not see the line markings on the other side and neither server could see where it landed on the opposite court because the sheet blocked our vision. We grudgingly realized that this is why the inventors of the game installed a net and not a sheet in the first place. What a disappointment! The evening was short and terribly frustrating.

But we were resourceful. We took down the sheet, went back to our homes, and decided we would snip this monstrosity into one-inch widths, one inch apart. This way, we figured we could see through the shredded sheet. The next day we put it to the test. Unfortunately, we ended up with a different problem. Now, we were always disputing with the opponent whether the serve went above the mangled sheet or escaped through it, just under the top cord. If I were the server, "of course it went over the sheet." If my opponent were the server, "anyone could see that it went through the sheet." Talk about diminishing hopes.

We somehow worked through that as we faced a more disheartening reality. To the utter surprise of our energetic young bodies, the game somehow seemed terribly tiring. The reason—we did not know that the outside lines were for the doubles game and that the inside lines marked the singles court. We had not bothered to study the rules and were playing singles with the doubles court dimensions. By the end of about twenty minutes we were puffing and panting and our efforts led to total exhaustion. There was no killer forehand here; just trying to reach the ball took skill enough. We headed home that night and considered tennis simply unplayable.

THE GAME IS PLAYED

NOT TO PROTECT THE RULES;

RATHER, THE RULES ARE MADE

TO PROTECT THE GAME.

We finally did the only sane thing. We asked somebody who knew the game to show us the basics. That is when we discovered how wrong we had been about the way the game was designed.

In recent years, I have often thought of that experience and how, within a few days of playing that game, we had gained insight of huge proportions. In fact, I would go so far as to say that the day one learns the lesson taught to us on that court, one has learned one of the most defining principles of life itself: The game is played not to protect the rules; rather, the rules are made to protect the game. That is it, plainly and simply. One would think that we would recognize that principle as readily evident to any rational person. All who have played any game would know that, wouldn't they? Yet the way we argue against strictures in life, one would think that life can be lived apart from rules. We castigate anyone who argues for the rules as if that one is engaged in something trivial and distinct from life. Is it any wonder that we get fed up and bored with life and yes, even exhausted by it?

Jesus made a statement on this same issue when some of the Pharisees talked about certain ceremonial rules of religious practice, as if those rules were ends in themselves. Jesus promptly reminded them that man was not made for the Sabbath; rather, the Sabbath was made for man. In that one statement, Jesus addressed both the legalist, who lost sight of living while trying to honor the rules, and the hedonist, who lost sight of the rules while supposedly protecting life, as if God's moral framework consisted of arbitrary mandates to make life difficult and to serve as debating points for the contentious. It was David, king and psalmist, who uttered one of the most profound statements about the laws of God. He said,

"To all perfection, I see a limit; but your commands are bound-less"(Psalm 119:96). The truths implicit in that simple dictate are extraordinary. "To all perfection"—by that he means that to every goal or attainment there is a destination point, a finishing line, a moment of consummation. "But your commands are boundless" means that there is an inexhaustibility to contentment when one lives within the precepts of God's intended purpose for life. That is what I like to call perpetual novelty or boundless wonder.

David's pronouncement is one of the most magnificent state-ments about why boundaries are set for life. He, of course, knew what it was to try to push back the boundary lines of God and find himself cornered instead. Having tasted stolen waters, he found out they were bitter. He traded a lifetime of regret for a few moments of pleasure. When he lived within the parameters God had set in place, he found out that the law is perfect, tasting sweeter than the honeycomb. His delight was boundless. G. K. Chesterton once quipped that before you remove any fence, always first ask why it was put there in the first place. You see, every boundary set by God points to something worth protecting, and if you are to protect the wonder of existence, God's instruction book is the place to turn. Anyone who thinks he or she can place the boundaries arbitrarily will either destroy the enchantment of life or else wear him- or herself into exhaustion. God's commands are there to protect what life is truly about, not the other way around. Implementing that truth in our lives keeps us from losing the wonder.

The metaphor of the game helps, but life is more than a game. We well know it is all not as simple as it seems.

"PLAY" BY THE RULES

Moving from sports and rules, we get another perspective from a playwright and poet. Shakespeare uttered these famous lines:

> All the world's a stage
> And all the men and women merely players.
> They have their exits and their entrances;
> And one man in his time plays many parts,
> His acts being seven ages.
> [Infancy, Schoolboy, Lover, Soldier, Middle-age, Decline, Old Age.]
> Last scene of all
> That ends this strange eventful history,
> Is second childishness, and mere oblivion,
> Sans teeth, sans eyes, sans taste, sans everything.[2]

Here, Shakespeare gives us a different metaphor to ponder. He borrows from the world of theater. Life is an act, played out on the stage of this planet we call earth. We put on a face, come onstage, and play the part that has been written for us in the script. This metaphor, I think, reveals why Shakespeare himself is known more for his tragedies than for comedies or everything ending "happily ever after." After all, if life is seen as a drama that ends toothless, sightless, tasteless, and "everythingless," there is very little left but to see life as "a tale told by an idiot, full of sound and fury, signifying nothing."[3]

While Shakespeare may have erred in his overall analogy of life to a play, he was right in pegging life at different stages. Here, I believe, there is a kernel of truth in how wonder is lost and disappointment begins. The first part of life sets the stage as the curtain opens.

WHEN IMAGINATION RULES

Where does one begin to define our search for wonder if metaphors at best hint toward something bigger? The Irish are known for saying the simple in a complex manner and they can be quite adept at it. The old farmer giving a tourist instructions on how to get to his destination illustrates my point. After listening to the question he shook his head and said, "If that's where you are want to be, this isn't where I would begin!" In other words, some retracing is needed before you will start to make progress. It is a little bit like missing your exit and discovering that you will have to drive another fifty miles before you can turn around to head in the right direction. So let us retrace the journey of life to its first stage, because it is there that the stage is set. To define wonder for an adult before seeing it through the eyes of a child is to miss the marvel of

> TO DEFINE WONDER FOR AN ADULT
>
> BEFORE SEEING IT
>
> THROUGH THE EYES OF A CHILD
>
> IS TO MISS THE MARVEL OF INFANCY.
>
>

infancy. I think we will find that though childhood is not the solution, it is the clue to the destination.

Childhood is that time when wonder is king, imagination is a playground on which one is oblivious of the rules, and one feels he or she is at center stage, undefined by a script. It is only as the curtain starts to fall that we realize how invaluable a part we played, even though we were completely dependent on someone else to give us our lines and the rules by which to play.

If childhood sets the stage then we had better be certain we handle it with care. It is a mysterious gift of dreaming that is completely at the mercy of others. Tragically for all of us in the so-called progress of civilization, we already know for a fact that childhood is shrinking and that it is we adults who have made it less than it should be. Children now have access to more that entices the imagination for a shorter period of time. So it is not that the day after is the anticlimax, but that the day itself has been shortened in its attraction. It is not "When do we get there?" that is now the question, but "Why do we even want to get there?" or "How long do we have to stay?" Nothing seems to hold us long enough. It is as if our brains are composed of packets of firecrackers that burst and last for a flickering moment and then we need a different explosion with a different sound and a different color.

This impartation has had such a devastating effect because now that child whose imagination has been aborted has become the model for adult receptivity. The span of delight that comes with the capacity of enchantment that was given to us as we began life has been killed.

In his book *The Disappearance of Childhood,* Neil Postman begins one chapter with the following illustration: "Vidal Sassoon is a

famous hairdresser who, for a while, had his own television show—
a mixture of beauty hints, diet information, celebrity adoration, and
popular psychology. As he came to the end of one segment of one
of his programs, the theme music came up and Sassoon just had
time enough to say, 'Don't go away. We'll be back with a marvelous
new diet and, then, a quick look at incest.'"[4]

To think that intelligent people can believe there is not something wrong with a mind that can switch subjects between matters
of such seriousness and such frivolity defies rationality. But that is
the point, isn't it? That is what has happened to us and that is what
we are imparting to our children. Fluctuating consciences, flitting
attention spans, diminishing reality, damnation by distraction are
what it is all about, all the bequest of the assaulted imagination.
Crowding little lives does not build options but, in effect, kills the

> BY FILLING THE IMAGINATION
>
> WITH SO MANY POSSIBILITIES
>
> WE KILL THE VERY DELIGHT
>
> EACH WAS INTENDED TO BRING.
>
>

wonder in all the options. By filling the imagination with so many
possibilities we kill the very delight each was intended to bring. We
really make a two-pronged mistake in giving so much so soon,

limiting the thrill of each. The first is the assumption that a child can handle abundance, and the second that boredom is cured by the possibility of more options.

I have been an itinerant speaker for nearly three decades. Today, after having traveled this globe a few dozen times, there are some comforts graciously offered to me because inviting parties in a sense see that as a veteran speaker, I have "paid my dues," and the comforts offered to me come on the heels of being willing to earn my stripes, as it were. But I have noticed something as I have witnessed the next generation entering this calling. Assuming privileges right from the beginning without first exercising the work ethic that they have resulted from is more hazardous for the individual than it is a blessing. There is a different way of putting it. Those who come by "riches" with hard work seem to look at riches very differently than those to whom wealth was handed on a platter.

That is precisely the way it is with the imagination. The imagination has been abused with the children of our time. Rather than wait until the imagination is mature and trained, the fragile capacity to dream and think is shattered by an array of "toys" so early that boredom is guaranteed. Watch a child with one toy and see the protracted enjoyment it brings. Watch a child with a dozen packages around and see the crestfallen look after minutes of opening them all. Is there not a lesson here?

Unruly Results

As childhood has been shortened and given so much, adolescence is now protracted and adulthood significantly delayed. In overloading the child years we have seen a protracted immaturity in the adolescent years. The point I want to make is not that we are entering into adolescence earlier. That would stand to reason if childhood is now shortened. It is the fact that we stay in adolescence longer. We dream less, we think less, we hope less, and we reason less, with more in our hands and before our eyes. The adolescent years have brought about the collision of rising expectations with a plundered imagination. As crass as it sounds, by the middle years, we are the hapless possessors of imaginations made impotent and we mess around with artificial means to return to the natural. Blaise Pascal once said: "Suppose the greatest philosopher in the world were to find himself on a plank hanging over a precipice. Do you not think that even though his reason tells him he is safe, his imagination will not get the better of him? Many cannot even bear the thought without breaking into a cold sweat."[5]

Such is the power of the imagination to defy reason. In reversing the analogy, our children have been placed at deadly risk as they walk through life's minefields with distorted imaginations and reason fails to convince them of the danger.

Somewhere in the 1980s, I picked up this quote. I do not know who gave it to me or who the author is. But whoever penned it had profound insight.

In the 1950s kids lost their innocence. They were liberated from their parents by well-paying jobs, cars, and lyrics in music that gave rise to a new term—the generation gap.

In the 1960s, kids lost their authority. It was the decade of protest—church, state, and parents were all called into question and found wanting. Their authority was rejected, yet nothing ever replaced it.

In the 1970s, kids lost their love. It was the decade of me-ism dominated by hyphenated words beginning with self. Self-image, Self-esteem, Self-assertion . . . It made for a lonely world. Kids learned everything there was to know about sex and forgot everything there was to know about love, and no one had the nerve to tell them there was a difference.

In the 1980s, kids lost their hope. Stripped of innocence, authority, and love and plagued by the horror of a nuclear nightmare, large and growing numbers of this generation stopped believing in the future.

To bring it up to date, I have added two more paragraphs:

In the 1990s kids lost their power to reason. Less and less were they taught the very basics of language, truth, and logic and they grew up with the irrationality of a postmodern world.

In the new millennium, kids woke up and found out that somewhere in the midst of all this change, they had lost their imagination. Violence and perversion entertained them till none could talk of killing innocents since none was innocent anymore.

Now go back and look at the list and see the progression. If the word *innocence* can be replaced by the word *wonder*, then you see how the slide into despair began. Wonder has a direct bearing on hopelessness and evil. The loss of wonder sets the stage for evil, until truth itself dies at the altar of a desecrated imagination.

Lord Beaconsfield (aka Benjamin Disraeli), former prime minister of England, once said something to the effect that youth is a mistake, manhood a struggle, and old age a regret. Interestingly, he never categorized childhood. Maybe if he were living today, he would say that childhood is a mistake, youth is a despair, manhood a waste, and old age a regret. In short, it is all reversed. We blow it sooner, we admit mistakes later, and just when life's enrichment is to coalesce into wisdom we give up the desire to live or imagine the past to be what it was not. Much of this has come about because childhood has become a mistake.

Unless we understand how to harness the imagination for what it was meant to be, wonder will die earlier and earlier in life. What a waste when wonder dies in infancy. What a tragedy when delight can no longer deliver in the virility of youth.

THE RULE OF THE STORY

Instead of a game or a play, we could see life as a story, a story with a purpose and with all the gripping reality of both tears and laughter, revealing the truth about life in particular and life as it was intended to be. If that is the way one sees it, there are building blocks at every stage and the wonder holds true at different levels of enchantment.

My favorite exponent on the theme of wonder is G. K. Chesterton. No writer in recent memory grappled with this theme as brilliantly as he did. It was he who said that he learned more about life from observing children in a nursery than he ever learned from his books on philosophy. It was he who also said that the older one gets the more it takes to fill the heart with wonder and that only God was big enough for that. Reading Chesterton, even his one-liners, is to see the truth captured in wit and wisdom. He drew a profound lesson from studying the nature of fairy tales where, he noted, there is always a condition whenever there is a promise or a reward: If you don't come back by such-and-such, you will become a such-and-such; if you don't do such-and-such, you will be turned into a tadpole or a pumpkin or be met up with by a big bad bear; always stay on "the yellow brick road"; do not believe what the "big bad wolf" tells you; do not build with walls of straw, because they can be easily "huffed and puffed" into oblivion. Some warning is always made to hold the attention of the young reader. Immediately, little minds are stirred and little hearts pound with concern over whether this condition will be met.

Our modern movies do the same, except they are more sophisticated and make the condition look even more "make-believe" than the fairy tale. We are able to see the crass and believe ourselves unaffected. We can watch killing and raping and evil and believe ourselves to remain uninjured and unmolested. In removing all sanctity, we have indeed created fantasy.

But Chesterton argues in a second reminder. Not only is there a condition in every fairy tale, but, "Have you noticed that the one to whom the condition is given never responds by saying, 'How come?'" Perhaps, he suggests, this is because if one did dare to demand of the fairy godmother the reason for the condition, she might just as easily counter, "If you want it all explained, tell me why there even is a Fairyland?"[6]

What a powerful argument he presents, gleaned from the world of stories. Fantasy does not mean unlimited possibilities. It is not a

45

game, but it has inescapable rules. It is not a play, but it has a script. It is not a tragedy if it follows the rules. It is unlimited delight when you know the author. When you play by the rules, you find out that Fairyland itself is not inhabited just by the true, the good, and the beautiful but also by the possibility of the false, the wicked, and the ugly. The story explains it but not all at once. The rules are there to protect the wonder of life with the grim reminder that it can all be lost in the face of many forces that seek to destroy it. Rules and script are part of the story, but so is inescapable mystery.

In other words, if we are to understand wonder we must see that the first chronological destroyer of wonder is anything that takes away the legitimate mystery of life and of living. The informed imagination contends that in displacing mystery one exhausts the pleasure. I believe that mystery is necessary if enchantment is to be real . . . and mystery and ignorance are not synonymous. This is where the story comes into play again.

Christopher Morley expressed this incredible reality in these words:

> I went to the theatre
> With the author of a successful play.
> He insisted on explaining everything.
> Told me what to watch,
> The details of direction,
> The errors of the property man,
> The foibles of the star.
> He anticipated all my surprises
> And ruined the evening.

Never again!—And mark you,

The greatest Author of all

Made no such mistake![7]

The years of childhood are filled with mystery. Evidently God does not see mystery as inimical to reason. In this day of cloning and genetic engineering we would do well to remember where to draw the line. Unlimited "creativity" that overruns the boundaries given to the "human creator" gives to us that which even God does not have. God did not give us infinite knowledge. When we pretend to be God and play God, we do so without the benefit of God's character and we redefine good and evil. Pushing the boundaries of knowledge without the knowledge of who we are makes the knowledge sought greater than the seeker, and only God is big enough to hold that supremacy. Wonder can be enhanced when reasoning knows where to draw the line, for the noblest reason is to know God Himself. This is a divine principle carved into the human longing for a story with enchantment. Ultimately, we will get to where that principle leads us, but before we do there are markers along the way we must first examine.

May I end this chapter by constructing a story that will help us begin our journey to recapture the wonder? It carries, in subtle form, the solution to our problem as we search for wonder.

There was a young man, living in a crowded village, always asking questions about who he was. No one admitted to being any relation to him. He lived with a family but they denied any relationship to him. They just happened to be his guardians. One night, as he tossed and turned in his sleep, a messenger appeared to him and he inquired of the messenger, "Who are you?"

"I have come in answer to your deepest questions, but I am not going to answer them now. I want you to get up early, pack your bags, and meet me at the gate that leads into the woods. I will give you what you will need for your journey. When I meet you, do not ask me all your questions at that time. You may ask just one before you start out."

With that, the messenger left. At the appointed hour, the young man was waiting when a veiled figure appeared, who said to him, "Take these three things with you, but use them exactly as I instruct you. This is a sword you will need, but it must never draw blood. This is the food and water you will need, but none of it should be wasted. This is the road map you will need, but you must only follow this route. If you get off course, this will not be sufficient to bring you back. So go on your journey, and Godspeed."

"I thought I had one question I could ask."

"You do," came the reply.

"Why am I going and what is the purpose?"

"Two questions in there, don't you think?" chuckled the stranger. "Never mind. Why and what always seem to intertwine, don't they? When you get there, you will learn not only why and what but also who. You will not be disappointed because this is what your heart is longing for. But remember, each possession is protected by rules. See you on the other side."

"You didn't answer my question."

"I did. God bless you, son."

With that the young man began his journey. He traveled through the day and slept at night. Each morning before he set out and at various times of the day he studied the map. Every now and then he would hear some horrible sounds and would stand guard with his sword. At other times he would hear the beautiful strains of music, but if he started to follow the sound he found it taking him outside the scope of his map. He longed to get closer to the music but he knew he ran the risk of losing the map.

Suddenly, late one evening he found himself face to face with someone who demanded his food and map, but the young lad would not surrender them. With swords drawn, they battled it out. The stranger wielded the sword brilliantly as he caught the young man's shoulder at one time and his arm at another. But every time the stranger went in for the kill, the sword tip would bend and not penetrate the young man's skin. The tide in the battle turned and the young man knocked the stranger to the floor. As he was about to pierce the stranger's side, he remembered that he couldn't draw blood.

He paused. "Why are you trying to kill me?" he asked.

"I just wanted your map. I need a map to get me out of here. I saw it fall from your pocket but, alas! It is in a language I do not understand. Be gone! I will wait and see if another comes along who has a map that I can read."

Retrieving his map, the young man continued on his way until he had a short encounter with a wild animal that came close to him. He quickly took some of the bread he had, threw it in another direction, and the animal went chasing after the food, giving the young man a chance to continue on his journey. He knew he had not wasted that morsel, for it saved his life.

Finally, as he followed the map, he saw a lovely little home that was to be his destination. He hesitantly walked up to the door and knocked. A woman opened the door, and as she did, she stared at him, first with curiosity, then with delight, and ultimately with wonder. She invited him in and knelt at his feet. "Let me wash your feet," she said. "They are dusty and tired." As she removed his shoes, she wept, because she saw the mark. A birthmark.

"Why are you weeping?" he asked.

"You will never know how much I have longed for this moment," she replied.

"Who are you?" he asked.

"I am your mother, my son."

"How do I know that?"

"The very mark you bear on your feet comes from me. Look! Here it is on the back of my heel."

"You are the mother who gave me birth? You are the one I have been searching for all these years? How did we separate? Why were you gone?"

"We will get to that. Did anyone try to stop you on your journey?" she asked.

"Yes, a man tried to kill me and take my map from me. But you know, something strange happened each time he tried to use his sword. It would not pierce me. The steel would just bend."

"Did you notice a stain on the tip of that sword?"

"Yes I did . . . a red stain."

"That was your father's blood. You see, that man, too, was once on a journey like you, but he left the track. He lost his map and now he speaks a different language. He cannot understand the map. Your father went looking for you, but this man tried to rob him to get another map. He killed your father. Once the sword drew blood, it could not be used again. With a useless weapon and a lost language, he seeks in vain to find his way back again. Only if he asks someone on the journey to take him will he find his way back. But he is determined to do it on his own, in his own way."

"So my father is dead?" asked the young man.

"Yes he is, but he waits at the end of our journey when we will see him again. For now, you and I are reunited, my son, and there is work for us to do. Let me take you to the house where others like you are now found. Some are returning to point the way. Some are working on the languages for the lost. Others are building homes for the ones who will return. Behind these homes are the graves of those who took the sword to blunt the power of any who attack so that others may come here safely. Come and see; they all have the mind of an adult but the heart of a child."

"What is the music that I hear? Can we go and listen?"

"Yes, in fact, you may sing with them. Listen to the words, son. Listen! And see!"

> There's a wonder of sunset and evening
> The wonder of sunrise I see
> But the wonder of wonders that thrills my soul
> Is the wonder that God loves me.[8]

"I believe this because I know this to be true. Yet, I have many questions, Mother, about my journey . . . and about my father."

"I'm sure you have, son. As we share a meal today, we'll talk, and this song will be beating in your heart as you listen."

"I can hardly wait. It's been worth it all just to see you. I was never more thankful for this birthmark. I could never figure out its purpose."

With that story, I begin. The search for life's wonder is filled with surprises, but it is also guided by conditions. If we understand the script and stay with the road map we will reach our destination. All that we need is given to us. When we reach our destination, our questions will be dealt with and the One with whom we enjoy the celebratory meal will bring the strains of the song in our hearts. The journey for wonder begins.

3

Seeking new sensations

while violating the sacred

first desecrates the self and finally

destroys the sensation.

CHAPTER THREE

Passionate Pursuit, Misdirected Search

HAVE YOU EVER BEEN ABSOLUTELY CERTAIN that you placed something somewhere only to discover later that it was never there at all? Or have you ever placed something in such a safe place that it is even safe from your memory and you can't remember where that "safe" place is? I never know how to answer people who, after listening to a sermon or two, will say to me, "You must have a photographic memory." One of the responses I have in my mind is to say, "It could be, but if it is I have forgotten where I have safe-guarded the film."

Memory is a strange thing. We all have fantastic memories for some matters and dreadful recollection for others. I have to admit I am always terribly nervous when, between my wife and me, we have misplaced something and I am tempted to say, "I gave it to you." The look on her face says it all. Invariably, it is the other way around, so much so that I sometimes wonder if she puts the lost article in one of my pockets after she finds it elsewhere. Not so, I'm afraid. I just lose some things and it is easy to insist to someone else that it was in their care when it was lost. When we add the component of mixed motives to unreliable memories we are forced to be less and less confident in the way we lay blame for what we have lost.

WONDER

IS ONE OF THOSE "POSSESSIONS"

THAT NEEDS DISCIPLINED GUARDING

AND THOUGHTFUL GUIDING.

If we are so wrong on small issues within the human context, how much more in error are we when we audaciously blame God for something *we* have lost while it was in *our* care when we had been warned to leave it in His care? Wonder is one of those "possessions" that needs disciplined guarding and thoughtful guiding. It is a tragedy that we so often go running after some new experience, thinking that the wonder we seek lies there, only to be disappointed. Then we castigate someone else for having duped us. Often that someone is God, and we cynically conclude that wonder is nothing more than chasing after a shadow of our own making.

Even so, I do not doubt that within the human heart there is some understanding of what wonder is when we talk about it, but it is one of those "better felt than tell't" states of mind. I have shared the concept of wonder across languages and cultures and watched as inevitably a light comes on and the person says, "I know exactly what you are talking about." A health practitioner told me once about a patient she had. On one occasion, just before that patient got off the examination table, the practitioner placed her hand on the patient's heart for a moment, saying nothing. The woman burst into tears. There were no words, no discussion. But at the touch of tenderness her heart cried out.

We all carry pent-up emotions within us and long for that touch that will restore wonder into our lives. But our estrangement from wonder is because of our misdirected search. God never placed it in some of the places or activities we love to haunt. Search as we will in those arenas for fulfillment and wonder, we will always return hurting and desolate. A brief glimpse at those pursuits explains much to us.

The Physicality of Seduction

I would dare to suggest that of all the places we search for the sustaining of wonder, most often it is in human sexuality. Few inclinations within our senses seem as mysterious and enchanting while at the same time can be so disappointing and hurtful. From the first realization of the desire to the enjoyment of it, we realize the intensity of the experience and the fragility of its nature. In sexual consummation, the mind and body go from inclination to participation to pleasure to ecstasy, so we think it is the act that delivers it all and forget the context that is needed to sustain the delight and take it beyond pleasure to wonder. Anatomically speaking, doctors describe sexuality as the collective firing of brain cells. That alone should tell us something. Pleasure and ecstasy are momentary and temporary. The wonder of it can be transcending and permanent.

I feel qualified only to speak of this as a man speaks, since I am uncertain about how to address this from the counterperspective of a woman. So if I half-fail here, I do so with full recognition that I am dabbling in a subject that is at once so important and yet so ridden with the danger of half-knowledge. Where I do feel qualified to address this subject, though, is that I have spent a significant portion of my life on the road and have seen firsthand both men and women making utter shipwrecks of their lives over this area. There is almost a sense of insanity that often comes over people

THERE ARE SOME

BITTER LONG-TERM DISAPPOINTMENTS

IN SHORT-TERM

INDULGENCE.

who are traveling, who feel freed from the accountability of family and friends to go on a spending binge of ecstasy, only to come away bankrupt of feeling and of wonder.

What is it about sex that is so wonderful and yet so destructive, so full and yet so empty? What is it that so stirs the imagination at the same time that it weakens the will and affects the soul? Everyone knows what temptation and attraction feel like. Many know what it is to give in to those temptations. And all who do quickly discover that there are some bitter long-term disappointments in short-term indulgence. I am sure that if we understood this we would be halfway to understanding why this wonderful gift is easily broken if trifled with.

GOD IN VULNERABLE TERMS

The Old Testament prophet Hosea gives us an insider's look into promiscuity and its cost. Hosea married a woman called Gomer, and they had three children—Jezreel, meaning "judgment"; Lo-Ruhamah, meaning "no more mercy"; and Lo-Ammi, meaning "not my people." Who with any reasonableness would name their children such castigating terms? "Judgment." "No more mercy." "Not my people." Only someone who has lost all hope in life and for whom cynicism has taken over. Such was the case when Gomer became a prostitute and sold herself in the streets of the city. Her marriage was left desecrated and her family in the throes of ruin.

Hosea repeatedly pled for Gomer to return. Can you not picture him? There he is in the brothel, begging his wife to turn from her debauched lifestyle and return to him and their children. His heart was broken, victimized by betrayal and agonized by the horrific extent of the betrayal. There were occasions when he succeeded in wooing her back, and she would return. She would ask their forgiveness and all would be well for a short while, and then the painful scenario would begin all over again. She would be seduced back to her life of enslavement by that lifestyle of intimacy with those for whom pleasure was the only measurement of an act. The wonder of sexuality was reduced to an act and a feeling of being purchased and used.

This Old Testament book is probably the most graphic in its story line. Hosea represents God, and Gomer represents the people of God. Their offspring represent the home or the society that results when life has been sold out to infidelity and reduced to the sensual. There is the gospel story in action and in metaphor.

In our society today Gomer is visible everywhere. Our entertainment industry recognizes this susceptibility and makes its profit from untamed passions and obsessions. The industry, of course, is not foolish. Those who control it understand well how to invade the thinking of the masses by offering the sensual and creating uncontrolled appetites.

As a young lad, I read the story of a wealthy man who knew that his untrustworthy servant was always on the prowl, trying to discover where his master had hidden his treasure. So one night he whispered loudly to his wife, "How good it is to go to sleep at night and not be afraid of losing our treasure. For who would ever suspect that we have buried it all in our front yard?" The servant in the next room heard this and laid his plan. He recruited some of his friends and one night they dug up the front yard, looking for the treasure. They worked all through the night, turning the soil over, but found nothing. The man woke up and smiled as he looked out his window and saw his front yard all dug up. The next day, he said to his wife within earshot of the servant, "How wonderful to know that no one would ever guess the secret hiding place for our treasure, buried deep within those bags of grass seed in our front yard. Who would ever think of emptying those small bags to look for it?" That night the servant and his friends came while the man and his wife were asleep and emptied the bags, scattering the seed all over the front yard as they searched for the treasure. But again, they came away with nothing. The next morning the man woke up and smiled as he saw the seed scattered all over the yard.

You get the point. The man got his lawn seeded because of the greed of the servant, and the servant got nothing for his efforts.

In order to be successful, temptation and seduction always require a disposition, an inclination, an imagination, and someone ready to exploit someone else. Vast numbers are deceived and duped while those who prey upon such dispositions smile at what they have gained and heartlessly ignore those they have used and left empty. This not only applies to the world of entertainment but also to our relativistic culture that, emboldened by "education," sanctions sexual freedom with an unblushing attack upon the way God intended sex to be enjoyed.

THE BARE FACTS OF SEXUAL FANTASY

Nakedness is a state of the body that is impossible without being affected by or affecting the state of mind. There is an indestructible link between nakedness and the mind. Nakedness does not just reflect that action of brain cells, an issue of pure science; it is a mind-set. Whatever causes a civilization to blush defines that civilization's values. The first time Adam and Eve sinned they felt shame, a new and strange sensation they had never felt before that took over their bodies and minds. The wonder of the garden and of communion was gone, and fear and suspicion took hold for the first time. Their first response was to cover their nakedness so that they would not be seen in that condition. To that extent, there was hope because shame is an indicator of a conscience that is alive. But why, one might ask, was there a feeling of shame in the first place? Was it not because God framed our minds to respond with sensation when sensibilities were violated?

PHYSICALITY AND SENSUALITY

ARE NOT ONE AND THE SAME,

AND WHEN THEY ARE MADE IDENTICAL,

THE REDUCTION IS FATAL TO THE SENSES.

In most of the civilized world today, covering the body is considered the decent thing to do. Anyone who wants to argue otherwise steps into philosophical quicksand from which there is no rational rescue. The arguer invariably invokes extreme situations from which to distort the normal.

A man and I were discussing life on the road when the conversation drifted to his appetite for things that in God's eyes would be a prostituting of one's self. I mentioned to him that in the scheme of God, the body in its natural form, uncovered, is a sacred reality and ought not to be trivialized. He snapped back, "By that token, a person should never disrobe before a doctor, either." A strange remark, I thought, but a reminder of our inability to see differences in purpose.

I asked him if he couldn't see any difference between a doctor disrobing his wife or daughter for his sensual pleasure and uncovering one of them in order to operate on her to save her life.

"I've never thought of it in those terms," he said and then added, "You're making me think, and it hurts."

I said, "You don't realize how many have been hurt because they have not thought of these things."

I believe that there is a world of a difference between the physical and the sensual. A patient unclad on a doctor's examining table is there out of physical necessity for the sake of the body's well-being. The physical is pointing to something greater than itself. The person lying unclad is not there for the medical practitioner's pleasure, but for his or her care. A sensual act, by contrast, is there for one's pleasure and enjoyment. Physicality and sensuality are not one and the same, and when they are made identical, the reduction is fatal to the senses. It is a different kind of death. It is the incalculable loss of the body's true worth and the death of wonder in sexuality.

CONSERVING THE ENCHANTING IN THE SENSUAL

The physical and the sensual have something to teach us. Think, for example, Why does food have taste? Why can't it be just nourishing?

That would be sufficient to meet our physical needs. A tongue without taste does not deprive us of life. Why are there flavors? Why doesn't everything taste the same? Why is there sensation in the first place? Why could reproduction not have just been an act, without pleasure? Life could still be generated. I truly believe that God has shown His marvelous creation by giving us pleasure in such unique ways. Touch with sensation. Nourishment with taste. Embrace with emotion. Sexuality with consummation. And memory so that we can retain and anticipate the experience. Mindless evolution could not have concocted such extraordinary connections and sequences. But this is where other heavy emotions weigh in. Unless the sensual is instructed and guided by the spiritual it descends to the irreducibly physical, nothing more than that. We see the irrationality of such horrific reduction in other realms; why do we not see it in sexuality?

Let me illustrate this from something radically different in order to prove the point. In the 1950s, John Howard Griffin wrote a culture-shocking book, *Black Like Me.* Prior to the writing, he thought he had a good understanding of race issues and was very vocal on the subject. He decided to take his understanding one step further and turn his white skin black in order to fully understand what it was to be black in 1950s America. He shaved his head and underwent a series of medical treatments that temporarily changed the color of his skin. His experience for those few weeks left him shocked beyond any expectation. He wrote at the end of that incredible experience, "I was imprisoned in the flesh of an utter stranger. All traces of John Griffin were wiped out of existence. . . . The man I had been, the self I knew was hidden in the flesh of another."[1]

Two phrases stand out: "I was imprisoned in the flesh of an utter stranger" and "the self I knew was hidden in the flesh of another." Such is the trauma when the physical becomes the only thing that defines a person and all treatment by others is dictated by a physical feature. For John Griffin there was nothing beyond that. He no longer even knew who he was because of the way he looked and was now treated. He had no other identity. "The man I had been was lost," he said.

THE ONLY WAY TO TRANSCEND

THE PHYSICAL AND THE SENSUAL

WHILE RETAINING THEIR ESSENTIAL FEATURES

IS TO BIND THEM TO THE SACRED.

A person's value ought to come from a transcending self that defines one's essential worth, regardless of one's shape or look. From that essential worth come relationships, experiences, memories, affections, and attachments. I know of no more powerful an illustration than this to remind us that if life is reduced to the body, there is no self-worth left and even the sensual will ultimately decay with the physical, leaving the senses unanchored. The only way to transcend the physical and the sensual while retaining their essential features is to bind them to the sacred.

None of the books I have written has involved me as deeply in another's personality as *Sense and Sensuality,* a book I wrote imagining a conversation between Jesus and Oscar Wilde.[2] Wilde was by all estimates a literary genius. His way with words and his creative capacity to tell a story are proverbial. Yet at the end of his life he lay in bed, dying in his forties, completely defeated by his own pursuits. One of his remarks about his own spiraling down is best stated in his own words:

> I started with almost everything in life that a young man would want. I let myself be lured into long spells of senseless and sensual ease. I became the spendthrift of my own genius, and to waste an eternal youth gave me curious joy. Tired of being on the heights, I deliberately went to the depths in search of a new sensation. What paradox was to me in the sphere of thought, perversity became to me in the sphere of passion. Desire at the end was a malady, a madness, or both. I grew careless of the lives of others. I took pleasure where it pleased me and passed on. I forgot that every little action of the common day makes or unmakes character. . . . I ceased to be Lord over myself. I was no longer the captain of my soul and did not know it. I allowed pleasure to dominate me. I ended in horrible disgrace. There is only one thing for me now; absolute humility.[3]

He went on to admit that it was foolhardy to try to obtain by one means what God had intended to be obtained by another. The logic is clear. God intends feeling to follow fact and not to be provoked in isolation, independent of the reality from which it springs. Feeling and sensation are the legitimate offspring of a real condition. That which God has joined together let no one put asunder. To seek wonder in sexual enjoyment apart from its sacredness is to plunder one's own body. To seek wonder through sexual fantasies is to destroy the wonder of sex itself. To do it God's way is wonder-full and lasting.

THE MATERIALITY OF SEDUCTION

Sexuality is not the only seduction to which we fall prey in searching for wonder. There is another, the seduction of money. Some years after he had won the lottery in New York, a man was asked during an interview by the media, "What has been the biggest difference in your life since your sudden acquisition of such wealth?" He paused, shrugged his shoulders, and said, "I eat out more often."

The laughter that followed revealed a strange but compelling truth. I have no doubt there were other changes—cars, homes, travel, and several other experiences made possible by money. But in the end, he was able to reduce it to food and choice. In a culture where the possibility of wealth is so great and the acquisition of things is so defining of success, we end up pursuing things that, even if we are successful, can never deliver what we envisioned they would. The reason riches become such a snare is because we end up evaluating life in mercenary terms and being seen by others in such terms, and life is just not so.

I was once privileged to deliver an address to the United Nations delegates at their annual prayer breakfast. Some time later one of the ambassadors hosted my wife and me at the UN. He was a fine man and extremely courteous to us. He came from one of the smaller countries in one of the economically fragile parts of the world. As we walked along those halls of power and saw some of the key world leaders hurrying by to their appointments, I asked this ambassador if he was optimistic about the world scene and the role of the United Nations. He gave a staggering answer. There was sadness in his voice as he quietly said, "I am afraid that in the end it all boils down to money. Whoever has the money calls the shots." That summed up the tenuousness with which we all live.

Each of us could relate stories of those who have much in the area of material goods but have lived sad lives. We hear time and again of people who end their lives as paupers when they began with abundance. As we are given glimpses into the lives of the rich and famous we find out that not only may one squander the abundance with which one has been blessed, but also that the presence of wealth is no protection against the ravages of the soul. Emptiness still stalks the rich, loneliness still haunts the icon, and disappointment still casts its shadow amidst the cheers under the spotlight.

I do not think there is a more telling picture of enchantment and horror than the wedding of Prince Charles to Diana—the hauntingly lovely bride, the pageant of color, the array of jewels, the carriage and the horses, the preening guests, the bedecked handmaidens and attendants, the pomp made to order for fairy tales. But with the exception of a few, none of the onlookers knew the agony within the young princess's mind as she knelt at the altar before a watching world and pledged herself to Charles: that the one who really had Charles's affection was seated in one of the pews and could someday wreck their marriage and crush her heart. Why, then, we ask, did

Diana go through with the charade? The coercive power of the guardians of our culture, along with the delusive disposition that she could override reality, imprisoned a life in its freshness of youth into a nightmare of deceptive trappings.

Such is the pitiful hypocrisy with which we all flirt, pretending that the cosmetic side of our day-to-day living is the real side. The truth is that the cosmetic side only hides the reality. Riches are a form of cosmetic. They have the power to buy the trappings, but they do not have the power to enrich the soul. A rich person can *do* many things that the poor person cannot do but the poor person can *be* what God intends for one to be sometimes more easily than the rich one can. Riches are to life what the IQ is to the student. It provides access to a higher degree but is not the means to being a better person. In fact, I would go so far as to say that great wealth is actually a great risk in life because great buying power lulls one into investing in everything that one wants materially, only to discover that material wealth is not all that it is cracked up to be. How does one live on the inside when everything one wants on the outside is within reach but has left one emptier on the inside than before?

In 1996, Oscar-winning actor Haing Ngor was tragically murdered in Los Angeles. Ngor was not a household name but he became known and respected by those who saw the movie *The Killing Fields*. Dr. Ngor was actually a physician turned actor who fled his native country of Cambodia after he had lost every member of his family to the murderous Khmer Rouge. This man had lived on wild roots in the jungle, hiding from his tormentors. He had been tortured and imprisoned by the Communists. When he escaped from Cambodia, he left with one precious possession: a gold locket that had belonged to his wife, from whose loss he was never able to recover. He wore that locket around his neck, with a lock of her hair placed inside it.

Arriving in the United States, he worked as a counselor in his own community and did an enormous amount of humanitarian work. He became an accomplished actor and was well loved by all who knew him. One night, a band of young thugs cornered him and demanded everything he had. He parted with everything but the locket and explained why. It was all that he had left of his wife's personal memory and he pleaded with them to not take it from him. They would have nothing of such reasoning because they had no imagination for such treasures of the heart. Instead, they mercilessly killed him in order to wrench the locket away from him. At the age of forty-six, Ngor died clinging to the locket, bespeaking a value that those murderers did not understand.[4]

THE ONE POSSESSING THE WEALTH

MUST KNOW ITS REAL VALUE

IF THE POSSESSION IS

TO BRING WONDER.

To ascribe value only to monetary things is to reduce one's own value to the same level. To lift the value of something beyond the monetary is to make it immeasurable. Once again, the spirit rises above matter if wonder is to be grasped. But our minds find it hard to apply. There is no wonder locked up in wealth. The one possessing the wealth must know its real value if the possession is to bring wonder.

The conclusion one draws from the seductions of sexuality and riches is that although they are wonderful gifts to have, they are only means and not ends in themselves.

THE SOUL OF SEDUCTION

Arguing against the seduction of sexuality and wealth is relatively easy because one posits the spiritual value against the physical and material and can easily demonstrate the difference. The loss of wonder is readily recognized in those contrasts because disappointment grips the soul. But the seduction of the spiritual is deeper and sometimes harder to grasp. For that very reason, there is nothing more dangerous in life than the belief that religion is the answer to our search for wonder. The seduction is stupefying and subtle.

Let me present a simple contrast. Sleep is a wonderful thing, but sleep itself is not merely a state of consciousness that bypasses the waking state. You see, when a tired body lies down and goes to sleep, it is the sleep of sequence. The fatigue of the body is carried over to the brain so that the body can recover from its expenditure. On the other hand, an anesthetically induced unconsciousness, though it imitates sleep, is the artificial effect on the brain that desensitizes the body. In the natural sequence, it is the fact and feeling of the body that demands sleep to recover, and the brain cooperates. In the artificial inducement, it is the manufacturing of the brain condition that disconnects its ability to feel and carries the body with it.

Religion is to true spirituality what an anesthetic is to natural sleep. Yet at the beginning of the twenty-first century, religious views are dictating world events and some of those views are as bizarre as one can imagine. The pitfalls of religion as a sublimated search for wonder may be too deadly in the end. There are people who believe all kinds of things; and in the West, we seem to have this very magnanimous spirit toward all things from the East, including the belief that the East has all the spiritual answers while the West is too materialistic. The truth is that whether the answers come from the East or from the West does not determine whether they are right or wrong. Truth must be measured by absolutes that do not change because of location. Even the great fighter for human rights, Mahatma Gandhi, was scathing in his attack on some religious beliefs of his own culture.

Growing up in India, one is both privileged and troubled by the abundance of religion that stares at us from every direction. Hinduism, Islam, Sikhism, Christianity, and dozens of other lesser known but equally assertive belief systems fill the land. One group, as a last expression of charity, tosses its dead bodies over a wall on the outskirts of Bombay for the vultures to devour. Another group packs up food and drink along with the dead to equip them for their journey into the unknown. One worships the dead; another denies any survival of the ego. One will kill to propagate their view; the other will put a mask over his face in order to keep from killing an insect. One fears the presence of ghosts that wander the earth;

another believes that he himself is only the body of another ghost. One philosophizes that all religions are true but will deny you the privilege of conversion; another affirms that all religions are false but necessary.

A highly esteemed Western philosopher of the twentieth century, Charles Hartshorne, celebrated his one-hundredth birthday in 1998. *U.S. News & World Report* titled a commemorative interview with him, "A Hundred Years of Thinking About God." Much in Hartshorne's philosophy I have a fundamental disagreement with. But when he was asked what his main reflection was after all of his thinking, he gave a very poignant response: "We live in a century in which everything has been said. The challenge today is to learn which statements to deny."[5]

Those are warning words at the very least. How does one know what to deny? To face the question honestly in the context of religion is to recognize that whatever else one may say about religion, religious belief in its most basic imperative controls the believer's world-view and behavior. I am not including the hypocritical or pretended belief in this statement; I am simply stating that if a person genuinely claims to believe something about ultimate reality and about what is sacred, that belief will control the person's way of thinking. Religion as a controlling influence has driven millions into huge steps of action. Killing, giving, sacrificing, submitting—all of these have been done in the name of religion. Most importantly, religion is espoused because it supposedly brings peace of mind, and because of that desired end, religion is used to induce states of mind that accomplish that end.

Look at the trappings of religion and you will see what it has done. Elaborate ceremonies, "necessary" rituals, sacred objects,

THE PLUNDER IS DEEP

WHEN THE SOUL IS CAPTURED

BY A BELIEF THAT IS

ROOTED IN FALSEHOOD.

protracted festivals, huge imposing structures, all of these have been used and abused to instill fear and awe into the consciences of people. The danger with this is that as these ceremonies and festivals and structures are woven into the fabric of one's routine, they gradually become part of a cultural expression until religion and culture become completely intermeshed. A collision course is set and emotions rise to the top with a vengeance because conversion has been made synonymous with a denial of culture. But that is only part of it. Ceremony lifts the mind of the individual into thinking in transcendent terms and the wonder that results becomes the source of meaning. I have seen this happen time and again. The plunder is deep when the soul is captured by a belief that is rooted in falsehood.

I recall standing within a few feet of a man who was participating in a religious ceremony. About one hundred long hooks were thrust into his body, and the tension on them kept taut by his handlers. Two spears pierced his mouth, from one cheek through to the other. Above his head he carried a huge contraption from which more sharp points entered his flesh. In spite of incredible pain he carried that weight as he walked for miles to the sound of wild drums and instruments while thousands lined the streets to cheer on him and the scores of other participants. All this is supposedly done without shedding a drop of blood to add the "supernatural" touch. Why was he doing this? To fulfill a vow he had made to his god in return for a favor. To push the question and ask him what kind of god this is who demands this kind of self-mutilation would be to run the risk of violence.

Such is the vulnerability of our mind. Think of the havoc the Christian church has wreaked historically by "selling" forgiveness and controlling the minds of people through guilt, fear, and confusion. Once the heart has been trained to submit to a habit it is hard to change because the repetition of a ritual engenders a state of mind that brings a sense of peace, lifting it to the semblance of wonder.

Different religions enjoin different routines—prayers at given times; the direction one must face during prayer; a language through which God communicates that has been given as a private revelation to only a handful in this world (any attempt to translate that language results in losing the inspiration); certain festivals, feasts, and fasts that one must observe at the cost of placing one's life in jeopardy; converting to another religion brings the risk of slaughter to one's family. Is it any wonder that any presentation of a counterperspective on God is seen as an attack upon one's culture?

What this all means is that spirituality for the sake of the spirit is not a sufficient reason for being spiritual. There are many traps in the world of religion.

Some years ago, I was speaking at a gathering in the Philippines.

At the end of it, a businessman in his mid-thirties asked if he could speak to me alone. As he told me his story he spoke in soft tones, periodically glancing toward the curtain that separated us from another room, because he was sure his father was listening and he was terrified that he would be disowned if he denied his family's belief. He was from India, a devout follower for years of a guru who is well known in India even today for his capacity to manufacture ash out of nothing and to read in your eyes who you are and from whence you have come. As it was his lifelong quest to meet this "sage," this man left his home in the Philippines and journeyed to India. The morning after he arrived, he rose up early to stand with the massive crowd in the hopes of getting just a glimpse of the teacher. For him, it was a dream come true to be within earshot and eye contact with him.

Suddenly, out of the blue the guru looked at him and said, "You, come up here and I will give you a personal audience."

"I was stunned," he told me, "and assumed he must be talking to someone else. So I just froze and didn't move."

A few moments went by and the guru looked him in the eye again, and identifying him by the color of the shirt he was wearing, added, "You, from the Philippines . . . I asked you to come forward."

That was all he needed. He pushed his way through the crowd and before long found himself in a private audience with the guru. I cannot disclose all that he told me, but here is the way he ended his story: "All my life I worshiped this person, and the moment came when I was alone with him. Here I am today some years later, disillusioned and emptier than ever."

The afternoon was hard and emotionally draining. But as I

shared Christ with him, he finally declared, "That is who I am really looking for." As we prayed and his tears flowed, his relief and triumph welled into a smile that said it all. Then he said, "The hardest thing is going to be not to repeat my daily offerings and not live in fear."

On a recent visit to Russia, I had afternoon tea with some dear friends. They are both graduates of Ivy League schools in the United States, now working as professors at Russian universities. Her expertise is in Russian art, and they both love the work they do. She befriended the owner of an art shop where some of the great masterpieces of Russian art were displayed. She would tell the man stories about the artist and they would spend hours discussing these matters. One day after she finished explaining a piece of art to him, he was moved to tears, and with his eyes moist, he said to her, "You must meet my wife." He went to the stairway and called for his wife and she heard him say in Russian, "Come, I want you to meet an American with a Russian soul."

I was so moved by that story, and I asked her, "What do you think he meant by that?" She paused. Together we sensed that he felt in her a genuine understanding of the pathos of his people: She understood their soul.

All these ceremonies of religion that we enjoin—from self-immolation to specific geographical points that control spirituality, could these be human-made means of somehow feeling we pay for getting close to God? Is that really what God is about? Is it not our crushed spirit and our broken soul that need His nearness? In Jesus we see how He felt the hurts and the needs of His people. A woman talked to Him once about religion. "Where should we worship? Some say on this mountain, others say on that . . ." So ran her concern. Jesus somehow got her to stop evading her real problem, which was her broken heart and betrayed spirit. He offered her a drink of water that would satisfy her soul. It is no wonder that she ran back to her village and told everyone, "Come and see one who told me everything I ever did. Could this be the Christ?" (see John 4:5–29).

He knew her through and through and drew her near to the salvation for which she longed. Religion and its specifics can easily lose contact with what salvation is all about. It is not about ritual; it is about a relationship. It is not about the posture of the body; it is about the need of the soul. It is not about the times of the day; it is about the timelessness of His presence. It is not about appeasing God; it is about resting in His provision. It is not about culture; it is about truth. It is not about earning peace; it is the wonder-working power of God. He safeguards that wonder.

I was in a Muslim country, chatting with the taxi driver, who was a very gracious man. He asked me if I was a Muslim and I told him that I was a follower of Jesus Christ, having become a Christian when I was seventeen. I could tell he was curious. Then I asked him if he had ever gone on a pilgrimage to Mecca.

"No," he said, "because if I did take that pilgrimage, I would have to become honest in my dealings as a taxi driver and would not be able to overcharge my customers. I couldn't support my family if I didn't overcharge."

There is the controlling force of ceremony without relationship. Jesus said, "No one can serve two masters. Either he will hate the one and love the other, or he will be devoted to the one and despise the other" (Matthew 6:24).

A question was put to Jesus once when the disciples, who were hungry, took some consecrated bread from the temple and ate it. It was a defining question and a tough decision in a culture where religion and ritual had become one. Had the disciples desecrated the temple and the bread by eating the bread? Jesus was put on the spot by the ecclesiastical powers who were horrified by what the disciples had done. "No," said Jesus. "I tell you that one greater than the temple is here. If you had known what these words mean, 'I desire mercy, not sacrifice,' you would not have condemned the innocent. For the Son of Man is Lord of the Sabbath" (Matthew 12:6–8).

In that one statement Jesus put our relationship with God in a direct line with our relationship with Himself. You see, the Christian faith is really not one that calls us to a higher ethical life. It challenges us to remember that by our own efforts we *cannot* produce a truly spiritual life. It takes the work of the Holy Spirit in us. That, religion cannot do. Ceremony has the power to soothe and mollify the conscience, but ceremony no more changes reality than outward behavior guarantees love. It is to this "greater than the temple" that we bring our temples—our bodies—and find in that communion with God where wonder lies. To violate that in the process of seeking physical, material, or even spiritual sensation is to seek a sensation without finding the source of wonder.

Have you forgotten what wonder is about? Have you been sidetracked into seeking it in all the wrong places? Have you even blamed God that you have lost it, or can't find it, perhaps? Have you ever lost a piece of baggage when traveling? If it was in your care, no one else is responsible but you. Had you left it in the airline's care, they are responsible and can be made accountable for it. The apostle Paul said, "I know whom I have believed, and am convinced that *he is able to guard what I have entrusted to him* for that day" (2 Timothy 1:12; emphasis added).

When you entrust Him with your life, He generates the wonder. Maybe you did not commit yourself and your longing for wonder into His keeping. Perhaps you lost your sense of wonder by trying to secure it in places where it was actually stolen from you. This may be the moment to pause and ask God for forgiveness for having gone after things that were not in His plan for you. To ask His forgiveness for a misplaced search may be the first step in turning around in the right direction.

When we lived in Cambridge, England, there was a picture in the newspaper one day that caught my attention. It was of a woman in her senior years. She was kneeling beside a flowerbed and facing the camera with one hand raised high and a smile that was as the golden dawn on a wrinkled landscape. You could not help but read the article.

The story was that this woman had been widowed for over a decade and a half. Shortly after her husband died she lost her wedding ring. She searched her house high and low but never found it. On this particular day, as she was gardening and digging up the soil to plant some flowers, she struck something. She dug her hands into the dirt, thinking it was a small stone, but saw something glistening. To her incredulous surprise, it was her wedding ring, lost to her for fifteen years. She grabbed it, held it high, and let out such a scream of utter delight that it brought all her neighbors out of their homes to see what had happened. A flood of memories bathed her soul. The ring brought back the feeling of decades of happiness spent with the one to whom she had committed her life, and she was filled with a joy that she could not contain.

If one ring, a symbol, can stir the heart to such bounds of delight, how much more when we turn in reality to the Shepherd of our souls and recover the wonder lost in our passionate pursuits and misdirected searches?

How do we recover that true wonder? That is the next challenge.

4

Enchantment in life

can never be realized in some thing;

it must ultimately culminate in

a person.

CHAPTER FOUR

Wonder Unwrapped

A HUNGARIAN MAN by the name of Andres Tamas was captured by the Russians toward the end of World War II and imprisoned in 1945. Because no one could understand the sounds he made he was assumed to be insane and sentenced to solitary confinement in a psychiatric detention center three hundred miles east of Moscow. His regular attempts to communicate with the guards when they brought his daily rations were dismissed as mere gibberish and ignored.

With the cold war over, Russia began to empty her over-burdened prisons and so the Russian authorities finally brought a Hungarian psychiatrist to evaluate this patient, hoping to be able to turn over the responsibility of his keep to Hungary. After some time alone with the man, the doctor stunned the man's captors by telling them that he was not insane, nor was he speaking nonsense. In fact, he spoke a little-known Hungarian dialect and was slowly being driven toward insanity by the treatment he had received from the Russians.

After the inevitable red tape, Tamas was finally released. His first request upon gaining his freedom was for a mirror so he could see what he looked like. He had been twenty years old when he had last seen his face. Now he was a man of seventy-five. He was so utterly shocked by his appearance, not seen for fifty-five years, that he buried his face in his hands and cried uncontrollably. He could not believe this was Andres Tamas, this withered, emaciated, abused man. He had been crushed under the weight of his tormentors, was lost to the world, and was now lost to himself. He could only sob, but his tears spoke a language beyond words. I cannot even imagine what he must have felt.

It is one thing to lose one's identity at the hands of others. It is incomprehensible to lose one's identity in one's own mind. How does one know what one looks like, or what one cares to look like, if there is no mirror to reveal the face? The loss of wonder and its pursuit in the wrong areas leaves one in such a state as heart and mind become more disfigured with every wrong pursuit. Thank God, we do have a mirror to show us what we once were, what we now look like, and what, by His grace, we may yet become.

The Bible is a book of simple clarity but also of intentional mystery; both are indispensable aspects of wonder. In its clarity, we celebrate our position as the pinnacle of God's creation. In its mystery, we are dwarfed. Every facet is critical and must be understood in proper terms.

The first necessary component of wonder is profound gratitude. Much about this state of mind we understand, but we commonly embrace so little of it. Charles Caleb Colton said of gratitude, "No metaphysician ever felt the deficiency of language so much as the grateful." It is felt in the deep recesses of our soul, yet it defies the speech of the most erudite. Benjamin Franklin said, "To the generous mind the heaviest debt is that of gratitude, when it is not in our power to repay it." That is what I am talking about, a debt that cannot be repaid even by the most generous. But though it is a debt, it is the only debt one can owe that gives one a sense of fulfillment. A gentle pressure applied to a strained muscle can actually hurt, although it brings relief. Physiotherapists will call that a "sweet pain." A debt of gratitude is somewhat like that—something that reminds you of your need, and someone who is able to meet that need for you.

But the word *gratitude* may need a little explanation. It comes from the same word as the word *freedom*. When something is gratis, we consider it free. Gratitude is the freeing expression of a free heart toward one who freely gave.

There are actually two basic emotions within the grateful heart. One erupts on the spur of the moment. It is unstudied and un-enduring. It exercises the heart as a momentary spurt of blood rushing into the blood vessels and then, with equal force, shrinks and disappears into a faint memory as it is replaced by other emotions. A raise from the boss! A new car! A generous gift! All those are wonderful things, but they are not really full of wonder. They can easily be forgotten and replaced by one unpleasant experience.

The gratitude that I am speaking of is not sporadic. It cannot be spent or exhausted. It is the transformation of a mind that is more grateful for the giver than for the gift, for the purpose than for the present, for life itself rather than for abundance. It values a relationship rather than any benefit made possible by the relationship. Even more, it is the capacity to receive, rather than the gift itself, to trust even when the moment seems devoid of immediate fulfillment. It is more than happiness. It is more than peace. In short, where there is no gratitude, there is no wonder.

A JOURNEY INTO INGRATITUDE

In reading the Bible, we often tend to overgeneralize our impressions. For example, we feel that the Old Testament is grim and regimented by the sternness of the Law that holds sway over everything. By contrast, we often view the New Testament to be lighter, more generous, and liberating. The truth is that in context, the truths in each beautifully converge, and in fact, there is much of both regimen and liberty in each. Let us take a small journey to examine the language of giving and gratitude in the Old Testament.

Right from the beginning we see the generosity of grace. In His covenant with Abraham, God gives Abraham something he never worked for and received merely as a gift. This is dramatized in Genesis 15, as we see Abraham put to sleep and the covenant-making God walking in the midst of the dismembered animals of sacrifice that illustrate the extent and certainty of God's commitment. What God is actually saying by this ceremony is, "May that be done to me which was done to these animals. May I be dismembered if I fail to keep my end of the promise." Yet it is utterly impossible for God not to be. God cannot possibly be dismembered. God eternally exists. That is how sure the promises of God are—His very existence guarantees them.

A few centuries later the land of promise is given to His people, the descendants of Abraham. God reiterated this promise to Moses and brought the people out of slavery as He had said He would. They harvested where they had not planted. They inherited where they had not toiled. They reaped where they had not sown . . . and they forgot about God Himself, because of whose mercy they had received all this goodness. God had warned them about this danger. In Deuteronomy 8, God said: "Take care lest you forget the LORD your God . . . lest, when you have eaten and are full and have built good houses and live in them, and . . . your heart be lifted up, and you forget the LORD your God, who brought you out of the land of Egypt, . . . who led you . . . , who fed you. . . . Beware lest you say in your heart, 'My power and the might of my hand have gotten me this wealth'" (vv. 11–12, 14–17 ESV). But they ignored God's warning and became intoxicated with their own achievements and successes.

Half a millennium goes by and you hear the heartbroken cry of God to His people through the prophet Isaiah: "What more could I have done for you than I have not already done? Why, then, when I am looking for grapes are you bringing forth wild grapes?" (see Isaiah 5:4 ESV). You see, God has kept His part, but they haven't kept theirs. The grief in God's heart is unmistakable: "What more could I have done for you?"

After Isaiah came two powerful prophets who represented to the people God's gift of love and patience in some of the most potent terms. The first, I referred to in the last chapter—Hosea, who spoke primarily to the Northern Kingdom. Yes, by now the nation was divided. The mangling had begun. The carved-up pieces of the animal no longer illustrate what may happen; they are actual. The nation is bleeding. The parsonage is the microcosm of the larger picture. The husband is a heartbroken man; the wife, a harlot; the children, born of adultery.

The second prophet came two hundred years later. Ezekiel's message is delivered to the South. God's plea through Hosea had gone unheeded and the Northern Kingdom had already fallen to its enemies. Now the prophet Ezekiel gives a different, even more stunning parable (see Ezekiel 16:1–14). His story is of a man walking through the land. Suddenly, he sees a newborn baby girl abandoned by the side of the road. Tenderly, he picks her up and washes her off. He wraps her in soft pieces of cloth and finds someone who is willing to accept from him the responsibility of caring for the child in return for payment.

Years later, the man is in the neighborhood again. He sees a beautiful young woman and realizes that she is the baby he had rescued so many years before. He loves her and so he offers his hand to her in marriage. They exchange the usual promises of fidelity and are married.

Now we see them some years later. Something horrible has happened. She has betrayed him and, in fact, has become utterly corrupt.

At the end of the story Ezekiel, speaking for God, gives the weighted application: "I was the man who walked through the land," says God. "I rescued you. I loved you. I gave you my hand in marriage. You committed yourself to me." One expects this to be the lowest point of his charge. But in the larger context of what had happened two hundred years before in Hosea's time, something more dramatic is going to be uttered.

"You've become worse than a harlot," says God. "A harlot, at least, justifies herself in her own eyes by saying that she needs the money and is paid by her lovers to lie with them. You are worse! You are paying your lovers to lie with you!" (see Ezekiel 16:32–33).

It was no longer that the nation had been seduced away from God, as in Hosea's day, but that she was now seducing others. From stumbling herself she was now causing others to stumble. Her deep disfigurement had been brought upon herself by her own efforts. She had done it to herself. The mirror was lost because she had thrown it away of her own volition. She no longer cared what she looked like. She had completely lost sight of what had been intended to be her life and her sustenance.

The journey continues. After Ezekiel brings God's message, the unrepentant South falls and another two hundred years go by before the prophet Malachi comes on the scene and retraces the last twenty-five hundred years of the nation's relationship with God. The book begins with God saying to His people, "I have loved you," and the people having the audacity to respond in a tremendous outburst, saying, "In what way have You loved us?" (Malachi 1:2 NKJV).

There we see it in all its shame—ingratitude. The entailments were obvious. They had concluded that everything about life was now wearisome and unfulfilling. Ingratitude had done its work, and wonder had been lost.

I must stop here and make an application, even at this point. I think of the nations that fit this very category, especially in the West and particularly, here in North America. We have enjoyed so much of God's blessing, yet people have forgotten God and gradually He has been blotted out of our collective memory. There are those who would like His name removed from the record completely. Even the one time of the year when the word "thanks" comes into our vocabulary, Thanksgiving, we now hear referred to as "Turkey Day." What an incredible reduction, from a heartfelt state of gratitude to celebrating a plateful of food. The heart has been displaced and the stomach is now the focus. G. K. Chesterton once said that to be thankful is the highest form of thought and that gratitude is happiness doubled by wonder. Thanklessness, then, must be the lowest form of thought, and ingratitude is discontentment, bankrupted of wonder.

Chesterton also noted that if a young child full of imagination has Santa Claus to thank for putting chocolates in her stocking on Christmas morning, have I, as an adult full of reason, no one to thank for putting two feet in mine from birth? Deuteronomy 8 is a grim reminder of what happens to a people who forget God's kindness, and who think that every success they have enjoyed is by their own merit.

THE ULTIMATE GIFT

Look back at what God had said through Isaiah—"What more could I have done for you than I have not already done?" It was Isaiah who first hinted at the answer. The giver was now going to give more. The provider was now going to provide the ultimate. The one who spared Abraham's son would not now spare His own. The author of life would now demonstrate what it meant to sacri-

AT THE CROSS JESUS GAVE

THE FINAL AND

ULTIMATE GIFT OF

UNMERITED FAVOR.

fice life. The broken body would be that of the innocent, not the guilty. At the cross Jesus gave the final and ultimate gift of unmerited favor. The disfigured body of our Lord was a reminder that even though God had kept His part of the commitment in the face of such betrayal, He would sacrifice His own lamb—His Son—as one last demonstration of His love. If this were not sufficient, nothing would be. That is why the songwriter says:

> What language shall I borrow to thank Thee, dearest friend
> For this Thy dying sorrow, Thy pity without end?
> Oh, make me Thine forever, and should I fainting be,
> Lord, let me never, never, outlive my love for Thee.[1]

Gratitude fills the heart when the gift has been understood, and wonder fills the soul when gratitude is expressed to the fullest. Edwin Arlington Robinson has rightly said that there are two kinds of gratitude: the sudden kind we feel for what we take and the larger kind we feel for what we give.[2] It is a very profound point, perhaps even better captured by Alexander Pope: "When I find a great deal of gratitude in a poor man, I take it for granted there would be as much generosity if he were rich." That is the crux of wonder. Wonder is best experienced within the context of gratitude. The extent of one's possessions does not change the quality of one's state of mind; it only multiplies the options for expressing that state of mind and heart. That is why gratitude is not realized by making comparisons with others but is expressed in the context of each situation. It is not whether things could be better or worse but that the heart celebrates the privilege of knowing the Giver who will withhold no good thing from them who love Him.

A. B. Simpson, a greatly respected preacher in the late nineteenth and early twentieth centuries, best known for being the founder of the Christian and Missionary Alliance, once wrote:

> Once it was the blessing, now it is the Lord.
> Once it was the feeling, now it is His Word.
> Once the gift I longed for, now the Giver own,
> Once I sought for healing,
> Now Himself alone.[3]

As I pen these words, I am sitting by the river Danube, overlooking the quaint and lovely city of Budapest, Hungary. About twenty inches of snow have freshly fallen upon the land. The spires of its buildings are all dressed up by this soft, icing sugar from heaven. I have just returned from dinner, where a quintet serenaded the diners. The violinist went to an old woman sitting alone, listening to the music, and asked her if she had a favorite song. She asked him to play "Somewhere, Over the Rainbow." As he magnificently played for her she began to sing with him in a quavering, sweet voice, overcome by her own tears as she sang, and I wondered why she cried. When it was over, the other diners applauded and the musicians, one by one, respectfully kissed her hand.

Was she a widow, longing to be reunited with the one she had lost? I don't know. But something happened in my own heart. For the last four days I have been in this hotel room to speak at some meetings and to write this book. But my suitcases haven't arrived, and I have no idea if they will ever arrive. My books, my clothes, everything I brought for this trip is somewhere between Atlanta and Paris and here. I have been restless and not too impressed with the airline. But all of a sudden, everything is put in perspective. The world is larger and more beautiful than my little struggle. There is a larger context. No, it is not that I can sit back and say, "I can bear this disappointment because somebody has it worse." It is the context of something bigger. Life is larger and longer than a single airline trip. I still have Him near at hand. I still hope I see my books again. But the context will ever remain the same and bigger than my immediate longing. That, I should never lose.

Rich or poor, gratitude can carry a heart through much, and wonder can still fill the heart.

THE MILESTONE OF MEASUREMENT

If gratitude impels the sense of wonder, truth compels the mind in its convictions. That is the second component. The world of a child may delight in the fantastic, but the world of an adult must move from what is merely fantastic to that which is fantastically true.

Anatoly Sharansky, a Russian Jew, is minister of trade and justice for the state of Israel. A few years ago, he and his wife visited his native soil of Russia, where he had fought so hard for human rights and paid so dearly for his efforts with years of imprisonment. He asked the Russian authorities for permission to visit the Lefortovo Prison, in which he had been incarcerated for so long. They finally and reluctantly gave in to his persistent pressure. When Sharansky and his wife entered that tiny space where he had been kept, he turned to her and said, "This is where I finally found myself, all alone, with nothing to live for except what I firmly believed in."

From there he went to a cemetery and laid a wreath on the grave of the noted physicist Andrei Sakharov. In a brief speech to the press, Sharansky said, "Mr. Sakharov put his mind to the cause of the nation in helping build the atomic bomb. But before he died he made a defining speech. He said that for most of his life he had mistakenly assumed that the most powerful weapon in the world was the atomic bomb. And then he said, 'I have now discovered that the most powerful weapon in the world is not the bomb but the truth.'"[4]

What a strong statement that is: "The most powerful weapon is the truth." Ironically, years before, in the midst of a world at war, Winston Churchill had said, "Truth is so precious that she should always be attended by a bodyguard of lies."[5]

The Bible repeatedly reminds us that truth is indispensable to finding the meaning of life and that the devil himself is rightly called the father of all lies. You see, all philosophy may begin with wonder, but it has to be guided by the truth. Wonder by itself, un-anchored in truth, cannot be distinguished from a fairy tale. In order to fully appreciate this we must first understand what we even mean by the truth, why it is so important, and we determine what is true. Let me begin this examination of truth with a simple illustration.

Some years ago when my family and I were in England, we decided to listen in on a trial from the observation gallery of the Old Bailey, the most noted of English courthouses. Unknowingly, we walked in on a case where a man, well past his middle years, was being tried for allegedly raping two little girls. The girls, being minors of about eleven or twelve, were not in the courtroom but were in separate rooms where they could see the attorneys and be seen by them as they were questioned through a television monitor. The testimony was not easy to listen to, and as it progressed I could sense anger building within me toward this man. What kind of human being was he to have subjected two young girls to this hell?

Then the defense lawyer stood to question the girls, one at a time. Taking off his wig so that he did not intimidate them, he began to speak to them very courteously and sympathetically, much to our surprise and satisfaction. His opening line was, "I want you girls to know that the most important thing in this room is the truth. That is why we are here. Do you understand me?"

"Yes," they answered.

"This means that all we really want to know from you is what truly happened that day. Do you understand me?" he repeated.

"Yes," they answered.

"We are not here to hurt you or to make this difficult for you. If you do not understand a question, please tell me. If you would rather not answer a question, please tell me. If it is too painful to answer, please tell me. We just want to know the truth." With that he began. As you can imagine, you could hear a pin drop in the courtroom. The accused himself leaned forward so as not to miss a single word.

As his questions unfolded, it became evident that the story lines of the two girls were headed in different directions. This was somewhat troubling, but we made allowances for that as they were children who had been through great trauma. Then came a critical moment. The attorney said, "Now I want you to listen to me very carefully. You actually told your parents of this incident about two months after it had happened. Is that right?"

They answered, "Yes."

"Is it true," he pursued, "that on the day that you decided to tell your parents, Mr._____ had seen you doing something you were not supposed to be doing and told you that he was coming to see your parents that night to tell them what mischief he had seen you involved in? Is that right?"

There was a tense silence and then one answered, "Yes," as the other answered, "I can't remember." From there on the questioning became even more troubling as neither physical evidence nor any other form of evidence was offered except the testimony of accusation. What emerged, instead, was a couple of young girls who had quite a reputation in the neighborhood for all kinds of pranks. We had to leave before the verdict was reached, and as we left, all five of us—three women and two men—were confused by the testimony and terribly perturbed that though it had appeared more and more that this may well have been a trumped-up charge, none of us was

> TRUTH IS A PROPERTY
>
> ASSIGNED TO ASSERTIONS
>
> THAT CORRESPOND WITH
>
> REALITY AS IT IS.
>
>

confident enough of the truth to come right out and say that it was a foregone conclusion.

Here is the point: One life. Two accusers. Life-transforming ramifications. If their accusations were true and left unpunished, what an injustice to them it would be. But if, on the other hand, the accusations were untrue, the man had been humiliated, and if he were convicted he would be censured for the rest of his life. What agony would have been unfairly inflicted on him and his family? What was the truth? The truth does matter, doesn't it? And if in one isolated incident affecting only a handful of people the truth becomes so important, how much more important it is to know the truth about what life itself is all about.

In plain and simple terms, truth is a property assigned to assertions that correspond with reality as it is. The key word here is the word *is*. That is why we all know the famous line of a few years ago by a rather infamous individual who said, "It depends on what your definition of *is* is." In a strange and ironic way, he was right. In dodging the truth, one may still affirm it. The luminary who uttered those memorable words would have done well to read Nietzsche. That noted nihilistic philosopher tried his best to deny the reality of absolutes but, in an incredible statement, dug his own grave. He said:

> The real truth about "objective truth" is that the latter is a fiction. Every candidate for "Truth" must first be expressed in language, and language is notoriously unable to get us to reality. Words, like a hall of mirrors, reflect only each other and in the end point back to the condition of their users, without having established anything about the way things really are. Truth is the name we give to that which agrees with our instinctive preferences; it is what we call our interpretation of the world, especially when we want to foist it upon others.[6]

Even had he stopped right there in his flow of thought, what an incredibly self-defeating statement that is. If what he asserts is right, his very notion that what he is saying is right is only right because he wants to foist it upon us. The statement itself would not be an assertion of truth. But Nietzsche was in agony of thought in wording that thought, and he did not like the reflection he saw of his own words. So he went on to add, "I am still too pious that even I worship at the altar where God's name is truth."[7] In other words, words are not merely utterances; they reveal something beyond themselves of that which we call objective truth or falsehood. The thing affirmed *is* the way it *is*.

From the perspective of our existence, the fundamental truth of our origin defines everything from there on. If we are the random

> THE FUNDAMENTAL
>
> TRUTH OF OUR ORIGIN
>
> DEFINES EVERYTHING
>
> FROM THERE ON.
>
>

product of atoms, then there is no one to thank for life, for nature is "red in tooth and claw."[8] On the other hand, if we are the handiwork of God, the psalmist's words ring beautifully true:

> The heavens declare the glory of God,
> and the sky above proclaims his handiwork.
> Day to day pours out speech,
> and night to night reveals knowledge.
> There is no speech, nor are there words,
> whose voice is not heard.
>
> —PSALM 19:1–3 ESV

Notice what the psalmist really does here. He speaks of creation as a language. A language not limited to one single group. It is a language that the whole world can understand. From that starting point he goes on to point out how perfect the law of God is and how pure His commandments, revealed in His Word. Taking the reader through the majesty of creation with a speech all its own to the Law, a written revelation, the psalmist ends by saying, "Let the words of my mouth and the meditation of my heart be acceptable in your sight, O LORD, my rock and my redeemer" (Psalm 19:14 ESV). From a language that requires no words to the Law that did require words, he ends ultimately with a commitment that would honor God with the word.

Yes, truth is a property of propositions that is in keeping with reality as it really is. That one ultimate reality is God Himself. Nietzsche, an atheist, played with words when he spoke of worshiping at the altar where God's name is truth. Gandhi, a pantheist, said at the end of his search for God, "God is Truth and Truth is God."[9] From different perspectives they both found it impossible to posit truth without using the word *God*. The Christian knows that in Christ the Word became flesh and dwelled among us, full of grace and truth (see John 1:14). If you want to know what truth is, look at Jesus Christ. He is the truth. He can never "not be." He always is. His Word is always true and He told us that to know Him is to know the truth. His being defines reality as it was meant to be. To know Him is to know the consummate expression of wonder. It is defined in Him.

> IF YOU WANT TO KNOW
>
> WHAT TRUTH IS,
>
> LOOK AT
>
> JESUS CHRIST.

Malcolm Muggeridge, who knew well the world of farce and make-believe often foisted by the media, said this so potently:

> In this Sargasso sea of fantasy and fraud, how can I or anyone else hope to swim unencumbered? How to see with, not through the eye? How to take off my own motley, wash away the makeup, raise the iron shutter, put out the studio lights, silence the sound effects and put the cameras to sleep? Watch the sun rise over Sunset Boulevard and set over Forrest Lawn?
>
> Find furniture in the studio props, silence in a discotheque, love in a striptease? Read truth off an auto cue, catch it on a screen, chase it on the wings of muzak? View it in living color with the news, hear it in living sound along the motorways?
>
> Not in the wind that rent the mountains and broke in pieces the rocks; not in the earthquake that followed nor in the fire that followed the earthquake. In a still small voice. Not in the screeching of tires, either, or in the grinding of brakes; not in the roar of jets or the whistles of sirens, not in the howl of trombones, the rattle of drums or the chanting of demo voices. Again, that still small voice—if one could catch it.[10]

Some years ago, well before the end of the cold war and the removal of the Berlin Wall, I visited the concentration camp of Buchenwald. It was the first time I had been in such a place. As I walked along the barren halls, I could hear the haunting echo of my own footsteps. I could think only of one line whispered by Dietrich Bonhoeffer, who was imprisoned there before he was moved to Flossenburg. Bonhoeffer was a German Lutheran pastor who spoke strongly against Nazi brutalities and against Hitler personally. On Sunday, April 8, 1945, as he was concluding a worship service for his fellow inmates in prayer, the door swung open and the guard barked out the words, "Prisoner Bonhoeffer, get ready to come with us!" Every prisoner froze with those words, knowing that they portended execution. Bonhoeffer leaned over and whispered to his fellow prisoner, "This is the end. . . . But for me it is the beginning."

Those words could only have been whispered by a man who believed in the indestructibility of the truth and that in the timetable of God, what had been spoken in secret would one day be shouted from the rooftops. The great American writer James Russell Lowell wrote:

Truth forever on the scaffold, wrong forever on the throne,—
Yet that scaffold sways the future, and, behind the dim unknown,
Standeth God within the shadow, keeping watch above his own.[11]

Ultimately, nothing can kill the truth. Our society lives with the fallacy that truth is an illusion and has put truth on the scaffold. But that scaffold inexorably sways the future, and in the day we all stand before God all illusions will collapse, leaving only truth standing alive and strong. If life is to be lived with wonder, even in the face of threat, then truth must be the indispensable component as living corresponds with God's design.

Fantasy and fraud die in the face of the fantastic and the true, in the person of Jesus Christ. Just as gratitude requires someone to whom we can be grateful, truth requires someone because of whom truth is possible. In both instances personhood is indispensable to wonder.

We begin to see a small flicker of light as we proceed in our search for wonder.

5

There is no such thing as free love;

love is the most costly expression in the world.

But the wonderful thing is that

it has already been paid for.

CHAPTER FIVE

Wonder Consummated

I N HIS BELOVED NOVEL *The Scapegoat,* Sir Hall Caine describes little Naomi, who, deaf, dumb, and blind, would wake up in the middle of the night, quietly walk into her father's room, and stand beside his bed. She was not sick or in pain, she had not been awakened by a noise or a dream. She just wanted to be sure that he was still there because through him she felt loved, cared for, and more than anything else, safe in the knowledge that she belonged.

Isn't it interesting how stories, whether old or new, sooner or later touch upon the theme of loving and being loved? It is a reflection on this vital need that we all have throughout our lives. We long to know and feel that we are loved. We long to belong in a relationship that is treasured, guarded, and growing. Nobody wakes us up to tell us that. No great tragedy is needed to prompt this desire within our hearts. I recall that as a young lad, no matter how anxious I was to play with my friends after school, I would stand at the bottom of our driveway from where I could see a good distance away to the neighborhood bus stop. My mom, who was a teacher, came home at about 3:40 P.M., and every day I watched until I saw her get off the bus before I ran off with my friends, reassured to know that she would be in the house when I returned from playing. Nobody told me to do that; no great brainwave fed my fancy. It was just the confidence that in her I had somebody special and I wanted to make sure she was there.

This is the third component of wonder—to understand and experience love. This, more than any of our yearnings, is desired by all, squandered by many, and distorted by most of us. Over the years and across cultures, I have seen the various ways in which love is expressed and longed for. It doesn't take long to realize that the longing to be loved is the same all over the world and that when there is the loss of love, rejection and hate surface. Rejection hurts. Hate destroys. Love builds. Love is a vital part of wonder. And love is that condition of the heart that "pumps" emotional intelligence through the blood vessels of life's daily encounters. It is the quiet confidence of belonging to someone other than oneself; a commitment to a cause greater than oneself; a relationship that makes choices apart from the self; it is the root and the progenitor of unending sacrifice. When that love is found, wonder is sustained even in moments of great fear. But the how and why of such a love is a challenge.

The Climactic Theme

F. W. Boreham, the English essayist, wrote an essay entitled "The Quest Sublime," in which he described the search of various disciplines for that which best captures the sublime reality of life. There are, of course, many that he could have identified, but he selected three: the quest of philosophy, the quest of science, and the quest of Judaism.

In philosophy, he takes us through the ponderous musings of thinkers with their singular ability to climb the ladder of abstraction. Volumes, debates, and arguments abounded in early Greece. They spared no verbiage in their attempts to transcend the physical and grasp the metaphysical. In the end they arrived at descriptions of gods and goddesses in squandered and perverse loves, in fact, in worse moral shape than humanity. Mythologies filled their pages, with seductions and betrayals at every turn. Truth became elusive and the conscience was still left empty. As someone said of ancient Greece, "The Greeks abandoned their gods not because the people became so immoral, but because their gods became so immoral."

A different route was taken by science in search of the sublime. This discipline set its gaze upon the heavens and tried to solve the riddles of the universe. Its readings expounded upon the marvels of time and space. But for a vast number, "staying true to their profession" meant that only natural explanations won the day. Science kept its sights on forces and laws and events. At best, some would concede the "footprints" of a designer, but the footprints they offered often did not lead the soul to satisfaction. It was one no less than Bertrand Russell who said that of the two deepest hungers he ever felt, knowledge and love, the latter one remained, at the end of his days, unfulfilled.

Then there was the venture of Judaism, one of the greatest ever contributions for mankind in search of the sublime. The Law was revealed to Moses; yet, in the end, the Jews recognized that the Law was only a mirror that revealed their flaws and disfigurements. It did not have the power to transform. The nation that received the Law found out how easy it was to disobey it, and in the end, feel nothing more than wretchedness. The Law was the main script, but the footnotes of destruction and death overrode the text. One prophet after another came to remind the nation of what she had done to herself in turning away from the Law.

In all three quests, it was not God who took center stage but some man or some idea that dominated the quest. Philosophy, science, and Judaism had not unveiled the sublime.

But then Boreham says that philosophy reached its climax at Athens when Paul showed its human limitation, that truth needed a source and hunger needed something more than bread. Science reached its climax when the Magi came to Bethlehem and saw not merely footprints but Emmanuel Himself—God with us. Judaism reached its climax when three young Jews—Peter, James, and John—were taken up to the mountaintop and saw Jesus transfigured before them. There, in that awe-inspiring moment, appeared at the same time Moses and Elijah, the representative of the Law and the representative of the Prophets. Both of them had seen and shown that the God of heaven and earth controlled the elements and was only fragmentarily revealed in the moral law. In the midst of that fascinating encounter, a voice came from the heavens and said it all:

"This is my Son. . . . Listen to him!" (Mark 9:7). The culmination of His message was not only a proclamation but it embodied the fullness of love that freed us from the burden of all our wrongs.

We often do not think of it, but here is the God of the universe speaking in familial terms about Himself: "This is my Son." Anyone who has ever had the privilege of introducing his or her child to another understands the joy when with great satisfaction you say to someone, "This is my son" or "This is my daughter." Something of the human heart is wrapped around that declaration. The very nature of God is declared in His introduction of Jesus. His is not merely a prophetic voice. He is not merely an emissary. He is God's beloved Son.

THE GOD OF THE UNIVERSE

DECLARES THAT

THE FATHER LOVES THE SON AND

THE SON LOVES THE FATHER.

Immediately, we see the blueprint for life even within the Godhead. God is in a relationship within Himself. This is not a God untouched by our emotions and our longing to belong. This is a God who Himself loves within His being. Theologians debate whether God actually feels emotions or whether these emotions are only metaphors for our understanding. This is not merely a metaphor. This is the definitive expression from which we draw the meaning of love and relationship. The God of the universe declares that the Father loves the Son and the Son loves the Father. "This is my beloved Son. . . . Listen to Him!"

THE APPROPRIATING HEART

To truly carry this love into the realm of wonder, there are twin recognitions that must be made. The first is that of truly believing in the gift of God's love and of His Son to us, more than as just an intellectual assent. It is God who offers His Son that we might become His children. We must know God's love in being related to Him, no less than a son should know the love of his parent.

The idea that God loves us can easily become merely a theoretical statement. We say it often enough, yet I am absolutely certain that even if this truth sinks home, the significance of it seems to wear off with time. We forget the immensity of the truth that God loves us just as we are, in the frailty and the struggle with which we live. Understanding this must more than inform the mind; it must stir the heart with emotion. That is the understanding that feeds wonder. When the truth remains abstract, the soul does not live off the treasure.

Let me illustrate what I am saying by contrasting it with the life of one whose name most of us have heard but whose life very few of us have studied, the English poet John Donne. To this day Donne is considered one of the greatest metaphysical poets of all time. Born in 1571, he made his mark early. When he was a mere eight years old, he went to Oxford, graduating with incredible achievements. At the age of fourteen he transferred to Cambridge. He went on to study law and was known for his wit and reckless living. Later in life, God got hold of him and he went into the ministry. He was ordained when he was forty-one years of age and died at fifty-eight. In that short period of time Donne became a familiar name across the literary and theological landscapes. When he was appointed dean of St. Paul's Cathedral in London he was overwhelmed by the honor and place given to him. But in spite of all this renown and of his acclaimed powerful oratorical genius, he lived with a very heavy heart.

Few know that the statue that bears his image standing in St. Paul's Cathedral today has a unique history. When a portrait was to be made of him, he asked for an urn to be inscribed. When the painter came, Donne wrapped himself in a shroud and stood atop the urn, to be painted as a corpse. There is not a hint of life, let alone happiness in his eyes. After his death, the chief residentiary at St. Paul's had a statue made of Donne and used the painting as the model. Ironically, during the great fire of St. Paul's in 1666 this statue was the only thing that survived the blaze. It stands in the crypt of St. Paul's today.

What kept the heart of this genius so heavy and unsettled? The biographer tells us that Donne once spoke to a friend and said that he lived with a terrible fear. Prior to his conversion he had written some blatantly blasphemous and obscene poetry to the woman he had secretly married. He knew these writings were somewhere around. He was haunted by anguish at the possibility that the recovery of any of these pieces would bring embarrassment and shame to the name of Christ and expose his own unregenerate heart to the world. This sense of guilt and fear may well have prompted the most popular of all his poems:

> Wilt Thou forgive that sin where I begun,
> Which was my sin, though it were done before?
> Wilt Thou forgive that sin through which I run,
> And do run still, though still I do deplore?
> When Thou hast done, Thou hast not done;
> For I have more.
>
> Wilt Thou forgive that sin which I have won
> Others to sin, and made my sin their door?
> Wilt Thou forgive that sin which I did shun
> A year or two, but wallow'd in a score?
> When Thou hast done, Thou hast not done;
> For I have more.
>
> I have a sin of fear, that when I've spun
> My last thread, I shall perish on the shore;
> But swear by Thyself that at my death Thy Son
> Shall shine as He shines now and heretofore:
> And having done that, Thou hast done;
> I fear no more.[1]

The words strike deep into the soul, from his soul to ours. Though a profound exponent of God's love, Donne was unable to bridge his mind to his heart with the full measure of God's forgiveness and love for him.

This is actually quite reminiscent of the father of the noted Danish philosopher Sören Kierkegaard, who at one time clenched his fist to the heavens and blasphemed God. He spent the rest of his life running from that horrible memory and even transferred that melancholic fear to his son. One can understand how, in sensitive hearts, the knowledge of having betrayed the God one loves is not easy to overcome.

But is not this the very depths to which God descends in order to meet us? Was not this the point of the shepherd leaving the ninety-nine to go and look for the one? The psalmist David knew what it was to blatantly dishonor God, yet it is he who wrote, "Blessed [Happy] is he ... whose sin is covered" (Psalm 32:1). Forgiveness that makes it possible to delight in the loving mercy of God should never lose its novelty if wonder is to impel life forward so that we are not trapped in the past. John Bunyan beautifully captured God's merciful forgiveness as he described in *Pilgrim's Progress* the burden of sin and guilt that Christian had carried falling off his back and rolling down the hill until it was out of sight. God has forgiven all! That truth from head to heart is the first portion of love.

Now let us contrast Donne with the hymn writer George Matheson, who penned a glorious hymn while in the throes of a bitter disappointment. Matheson dearly loved a woman whom he wanted to marry. As the romance developed he knew he had to tell her that he was going blind before her love for him went any deeper. To his total surprise, she broke up the relationship. Although he felt something within him had died, the hymn that he wrote was then born in his soul: "I had the impression of having it dictated to me by some inward voice, rather than of working it out myself."[2]

O Love that wilt not let me go,
I rest my weary soul in thee;
I give thee back the life I owe,
That in thine ocean depths its flow
May richer, fuller be.

O joy that seekest me through pain,
I cannot close my heart to thee;
I trace the rainbow through the rain,
And feel the promise is not vain
That morn shall tearless be.[3]

Through this great loss, he nevertheless lived confidently in the conviction that though everyone else might reject him, God would never reject him. Two poets, two songwriters, two great thinkers. For one, doubt and fear overrode the reality of his forgiveness. For the other, truth had sunk into the heart and he basked in a love that would never let him go.

ONLY GOD IS ABLE TO

HUMBLE US WITHOUT

HUMILIATING US AND TO

EXALT US WITHOUT FLATTERING US.

Unless the love of God is clasped close to the heart it can never give birth to this kind of confidence. Was it not this same daring courage on the part of the prostitute who walked into the Pharisee's home and lavished her ointment and tears upon our Lord, just to express the joy of her forgiveness? Love's first step is to believe and receive fully God's mercy. I once read somewhere that only God is able to humble us without humiliating us and to exalt us without flattering us. That is what His forgiveness accomplishes.

But there is a second step. As wonder-filled as love is, and as gracious as its provider is, the cost of love is also most fearsome. We all know what it is to need, to long, to want, to feel. Our songs sing of that kind of love. We listen over the air or in shopping centers or in elevators—the songs all have a similar strain to them. It is all about what we want and wish and plead for. But here we lose our way. It has been a long time since I have heard a song about the cost of love and about what it really means to love. The extraordinary thing about love, as Jesus described it, is not merely in the wonder that He loves us but in the exhaustiveness of the cost of His love. Like any great portion of wealth, it brings its returns in proportion to its investment.

Years ago, J. H. Oldham wrote a book titled *Life Is Commitment,* in which he said, "There are some things in life, and they may be the most important things, that we cannot know by research or reflection, but only by committing ourselves. We must dare in order to know. Life is full of situations to which I can respond not with part of myself but only with commitment of my whole being."[4]

And that, may I add, is the essential component of love that in turn feeds wonder. What it costs determines what it brings. Only a commitment lived out understands what love means.

Love is greater than any law. The whole Law given at first to Moses came in about 613 precepts. These revealed the parameters in which God prescribed authentic worship. One cannot but be over-whelmed by the sheer weight of obligation. About half a century later David, in the fifteenth Psalm, takes these 613 precepts and reduces them to about 11. Two centuries later, Isaiah shrinks them to 6. Micah takes those 6 and summarizes them into 3. Habakkuk takes Micah's 3 and crystallizes them down to 1 command: "The just shall live by faith."[5]

EVERYTHING IN THE TWO TESTAMENTS

THAT POINTS TO THE MORAL,

POINTS TO THE SUPREMACY

OF KNOWING GOD'S LOVE.

It is interesting to see the apostle Paul, who well understood what faith meant (in fact, three times in his epistles Paul quotes that passage from Habakkuk), take that one precept and fine-tune it into one idea. The great expressions of the truly spiritual life, he said, are faith, hope, and love. But the greatest expression, he said, even greater than faith, the final precept that Habakkuk taught, the greatest expression is love. Paul's entire treatment is to show how love expresses itself, not how love is enjoyed (see 1 Corinthians 13). Jesus also took that hunger of the heart and combined it with the demands of the Law. The greatest commandment, he said, was to "Love the Lord your God with all your heart and strength and soul and mind and your neighbors as yourselves. On this precept," He said, hang "all the Law and the Prophets" (Matthew 22:37–40). Everything in the two Testaments that points to the moral also points to the supremacy of knowing God's love, the key to unlocking life's treasure.

THE QUINTESSENTIAL DEMONSTRATION

English is somewhat impoverished when it comes to the language of love. I am sure we are all probably familiar with C. S. Lewis's popular treatment of the theme from the Greek language, which in English he entitled "Four Loves." *Agape,* as the purest love, is best represented by the love of God. *Phileo,* friendship love, is best exemplified in a love shared between friends. *Storge,* a protective love, is best seen in that of a parent for child. Finally, *eros,* which is romantic love, is best captured in marriage. These four words have a wider range than the one captured by our one English word *love.*

However, two things are recognized with age: that the true nature of romance is much deeper than sexuality *(eros)* and that protective love *(storge),* as wonderful as it is, cannot keep us from some losses over time. Health and life itself come into jeopardy. This is where all the pointers to knowing God take on great significance and where what it means to love Him and be loved by Him is put to the test.

One of the last conversations in Jesus' earthly life brings this all together. Let me take you to a scene in the New Testament. Jesus has experienced a series of betrayals and speaks to one of His disciples in a profound encounter. First, it was the temple authorities themselves who did not care for His strong reminder that true religion was one of heart. They had torn the law on paper apart from the law imprinted on the heart, and they would use the law to kill Him, to crucify *Agape*.

A few days later the disciples were unable to stay awake and care for Him when He needed them most. They left Him alone—*storge* absent. Then it was Judas who dared to betray Jesus with a kiss. He used a symbol of friendship with which to betray his love, and *phileo* was made commonplace.

Finally, there was Peter, who when he was challenged, denied that he even knew Him. This was the same man who had bragged that others might betray Jesus but not he. His denial took place three times. All three of the loves demanded at the moment were conspicuously absent in the disciple into whom Jesus had poured so much. In one of the most moving passages of the New Testament, Jesus appears to Peter after His death and resurrection from the dead, and in that encounter, these three concepts for love emerge.

Jesus says to him, "Peter, do you love *[agape]* me?" Peter answers, "Lord, I love *[phileo]* you." Why is it that Peter does not use the same word Jesus does? I wonder. It would be like my son asking me, "Dad, do you love me?" and me answering, "You know that I am fond of you." A strange response, don't you think? Jesus, therefore, repeats with added intensity, "Peter, do you *really* love *[agape]* me? Peter answers again with his own terminology, "Lord, you know that I love *[phileo]* you." Jesus now tries Peter's word. "Peter, do you love *[phileo]* me?"

It seems to me that Peter is running from the loftiness of the question and Jesus finally brings him face to face with his own heart

> HOW DOES ONE ENJOY LOVE?
>
> BY BEING TOTALLY SOLD OUT
>
> IN THE HEART
>
> TO GOD HIMSELF.
>
>

and pushes the question. In effect, He is saying, "Are you really even a friend to me, Peter?" (see John 21:15–17).

True love is a thing of the heart and must be raised to what God intends it to be. It can never be fully expressed until it has been totally given first to God. The illustration is so vividly put before us. We see Jesus' personal love for this disciple. Time and again Peter had failed. He stumbled, bungled, and overestimated his own commitment, and yet there is a tenderness that Jesus shows toward Peter that is proverbial. But having known forgiveness, Peter missed love's second step—to give himself fully to that love. "Peter, do you really love me?" That was the question. Only in the binding of one's will can love be truly expressed. Jesus reminded Peter of this. He in effect told Peter that the day would come when he would have to prove his love by his willingness to lay down his life for his Lord. How does one enjoy love? By being totally sold out in the heart to God Himself.

Of all the disciples who floundered and stumbled, Peter was at the forefront. Yet it was to him that Jesus issued that pastoral call:

"Feed my sheep." Wonder is experienced in forgiveness. Wonder is enjoyed in total commitment and in being called to serve.

THE PRESENT CONFIDENCE

The last component of wonder, as I see it, is a convinced sense of security, both in being able to accept yourself as you are and in having confidence that God has conquered not only life but also death. That twin knowledge keeps the heart at rest and hope fanned in the soul.

In his address to the Athenian philosophers the apostle Paul made a definitive statement about God's plan for the ages: "From one man he made every nation of men, that they should inhabit the whole earth; and he determined the times set for them and the exact places where they should live. God did this so that men would seek him and perhaps reach out for him and find him, though he is not far from each one of us" (Acts 17:26–27).

Paul says that every race and culture was present in God's mind before He created them and gave them their territories on earth. God positioned each of us in a particular race and yet Paul reminds us that not just as part of our race but as an individual, He is not far from any one of us. This assurance that God planned the very core of my personality, that I was purposefully born and fashioned according to God's plan, and that He is near to me wherever I am is reason to celebrate the way He has, to use the colloquial, "wired me." It is easy in a vast world with a diversity of giftedness to forget that God has a personal concern in my life.

I often think of the context into which John Wesley was born.

He was one of nineteen children. His mother, Susannah, was herself the twenty-fifth child of her mother. How does one who is number twenty-five and brings forth nineteen more find the answer to individuality? Yet she was determined from the time she was a young mother that every child would have his or her time alone with her. She laid a plan and followed that plan. It was no accident that as a child, young John had learned that he was important as an individual. On the day that his heart was turned toward his call, that very morning, he opened his Bible and read: "You are not far from the kingdom." One life . . . not far from the kingdom. He recognized his inheritance as an individual and as a son of the King and opened his heart to all that God had for him.

Until we see in ourselves the uniqueness of God's touch, we will always want to be someone else and will live under the illusion that being someone else would be better. History is full of examples of God using the most unlikely people for His extraordinary purposes. One of the most extraordinary stories of God's unexpected favor is the story of William Cowper. He was, by all descriptions, not pleasant to look at. Slight of figure, he had a pale, distorted face and swollen eyes with dark rings around them. One biographer described him as "a quivering little bundle of nerves." On several occasions he was sent to an insane asylum for treatment. At night he would pull the covers over his face when he went to sleep, lest he draw the attention of the spirits that he feared flitted across the wall in the dark. His lone champion who had any hopes for his future, his mother, died very suddenly, leaving him grief-stricken. She was the subject of much of his poetry throughout his life, such as the following:

I heard the bell toll'd on thy burial day;
I saw the hearse that bore thee slow away
Thus many a sad tomorrow came and went,
Till all my stock of infant sorrow spent.[6]

His grief knew no bounds, but his mother's prayers asking God to use him had soared to the heavens. And as God saw fit, Cowper ended up as minister of music at Olney, England, coauthoring a book of hymns with the pastor, who was none other than converted slave trader John Newton. The best known of Cowper's hymns may well be:

God moves in a mysterious way, His wonders to perform;
He plants His footsteps in the sea and rides upon the storm.

His purposes will ripen fast, unfolding every hour;
The bud may have a bitter taste, but sweet will be the flower.

Blind unbelief is sure to err and scan His works in vain;
God is His own interpreter, and He will make it plain.[7]

It is an incredible tribute to the love and grace of God that these lines were penned by a man of whom his eulogist said:

O poets, from a maniac's tongue was poured the deathless singing.
O Christians, at your Cross of hope a hopeless hand was clinging!
O men, this man in brotherhood your weary paths beguiling,
Groaned inly while he taught you peace,
   and died while you were smiling.[8]

The "maniac" has brought consolation to millions by making it possible for them to sing. His life, though so painfully spent, has brought comfort to many a hopeless heart. So should it be with us. To believe that He has made you uniquely, debilitated or not, and with a distinctive touch, is to celebrate the uniqueness of every individual life. In the vastness of God's creation, your birth and your reach is something unique. With the psalmist we may personalize it and say, "What is there in me that you take notice of me?" (see Psalm 8:4). But again with the psalmist we can also say, "You knit me together in my mother's womb. . . . I am fearfully and wonderfully made" (Psalm 139:13–14).

> Earth's crammed with heaven,
> and every common bush afire with God
> But only he who sees, takes off his shoes
> The rest sit round it and pluck blackberries.[9]

Part of wonder is to recognize that heaven has been crammed into every life by the marvelous hand of the Creator.

THE CONSUMMATION OF IT ALL

Not only is wonder attached to my individual uniqueness but there is also an eternal perspective. By rising from the dead, Jesus confirms within your heart and mine that while surrounded by death and the limitations of time, there is a reality that stretches beyond the now to the very presence of God. The wonder of time can only be understood in eternity. That truth is so rich in its intent and content and gives promise and hope to the Christian faith.

I was once asked in an open forum to define and describe heaven. There was silence as the audience first chuckled and then waited with bated breath to see what I would say. Heaven is one of those states for which any analogy falls short, but hints are given that present a meaningful expression of what it would mean to be in heaven.

THE EXISTENTIAL LONGING

FOR THE ULTIMATE

IN BEAUTY AND SERENITY—

THAT IS HEAVEN.

I find it so interesting that hell is not hard to illustrate. Our daily experience points to so much of hell on earth. Heaven is also not hard to illustrate when we think of it in terms of what it is not—no death, no tears, no pain. To describe what it is strains the vocabulary and challenges the imagination.

Do you remember what C. S. Lewis said about heaven in *The Weight of Glory?*

In speaking of this desire for our own far off country, which we find in ourselves even now, I feel a certain shyness. I am almost committing an indecency. I am trying to rip open the inconsolable secret in each one of you—The secret which hurts so much that you take your revenge on it by calling it names like Nostalgia and Romanticism and Adolescence; The secret also which pierces with such sweetness that when, in very intimate conversation, the mention of it becomes imminent, we grow awkward and affect to laugh at ourselves; The secret we cannot hide and cannot tell, though we desire to do both. We cannot tell it because it is a desire for something that has never actually appeared in our experience. We cannot hide it because our experience is constantly suggesting it, and we betray ourselves like lovers at the mention of a name.[10]

The existential longing for the ultimate in beauty and serenity—that is heaven. That is what gives us hope, even now. But I believe the best description of heaven is given in a different word, other than just the negatives. I will get to that.

To start with, knowing what it means to live by essence and not by function—what it means to *be,* apart from what it means to *do*—nudges open the door of understanding. It is impossible to understand life until we know what it is to really "be." Ask anyone today who they are and invariably the answer drifts to one's profession or skill. And then our treatment of the individual results from that. Heaven is that reality where your existence is lived to its fullest essence and the God who fashioned you leads you to the ultimate expression for which He made you. We talk of heaven as a place—and it is that. We talk of heaven as a feeling—and it is that. We talk of heaven as a destiny—and it is that. But it is more. I capture this sense of being in three words.

The first is in the sense of *touch*. You see, the most defining aspect of heaven is the kind of existence when every sense converges and coalesces to make the presence of God touch us in a way we cannot be touched now. In the human body, touch is a critical sensation. We know so much through touch, both of love and pain.

When a person dies he or she looks the same outwardly but there is no response to touch. We say that it is because the brain is dead and there is no neurological activity to transmit sensation. When the body was alive, touch was a means to point to something else. If it hurt, you knew there was something wrong with that part of the body. When you felt good, the touch made you reach and touch in return. Touch becomes definitive. When you are regenerated by the Holy Spirit of God, God has touched your soul. Every hunger, every sensation points to the need to feel His presence more and more.

Right now those hungers are not fully satisfied and they are weaknesses because the flesh that ensnares us is the very flesh that wants to feel. Right now our strengths and weaknesses are impeded by the sheer weight of material existence and by sensuality. Then the final act of physicality takes place—death.

But at death, for the Christian, everything that was a longing but was restricted by the flesh is now fulfilled in the spirit. The touch that was longed for externally is now internal. The faith that pointed to the future is now an eternal realm.

This leads us to the second word—*sight*. In heaven, faith becomes sight. We see His presence in a way that our earthly being can never envision. Jesus uses the realm of sight as a key and the realm of touch as a test. After Thomas had touched His risen body

Jesus said to him, "Because you have *seen* me, you have believed; blessed are those who have *not* seen and yet have believed" (John 20:29; emphasis added). The key word here is *blessed,* which conveys more than the concept of happiness.

Jesus had addressed this earlier as a promise in which we are introduced to the third word: "Blessed are the *pure* in heart for they will *see* God" (Matthew 5:8; emphasis added). Jesus introduced here the one aspect that is indispensable to the full enjoyment of sight and touch—*purity.* The greatest use of that word in the Old Testament is in the Book of Exodus and the Book of 1 Kings. In Exodus it occurs in the instructions for the building the tabernacle, where God said He would dwell with them. The material that was to be used in building the tabernacle was to be pure. In the Book of 1 Kings it is used in the instructions for building the temple, where God said He would meet with them. Everything that was to be used in building the temple was to be pure. In the New Testament the word *pure* occurs most in the Book of Revelation when John "sees" the heavenly future.

LIKE A CHILD WHO SUDDENLY STOPS SOBBING

WHEN HE IS CLASPED IN THE ARMS OF HIS MOTHER,

SUCH WILL BE THE GRIP OF

HEAVEN UPON OUR SOULS.

RECAPTURE THE WONDER

The word *see* occurs scores of times. In that enchanting vision, John is astounded that what he sees in heaven is that there is no temple there. Where would God "dwell," where would He "meet" with His people? Watch now the coalescing. Sight becomes pre-eminent as he sees the majesty of God face to face. God's voice is heard, His presence is seen, and John feels the touch of God. The "glaucoma" of the soul is gone. The "thaumas," that is, the wonder, now sees and touches and recognizes. He now knows God as he is known, the marvelous coalescing of senses. There is purity in the encounter—a purified heart that has known the purest touch in his spirit, a pure relationship, seeing the purest of all and hearing the pure voice of God. That is what heaven is—we are in the presence of God, the limitations of the flesh are gone, and we are fulfilled by the pure encounter of our spirits with God. It is the consummation of wonder then, when sight and hope combine and touch is sublimely felt by God's presence in direct encounter with the soul. Like a child who suddenly stops sobbing when he is clasped in the arms of his mother, such will be the grip of heaven upon our souls.

Hall Caine's story of Naomi concludes with the reminder that in the end she could hear, talk, see, speak, and touch her father's face. That was what she needed. That was the most sublime truth to her.

You see, sublimity can never be attained in relation to an idea; it can only come in relation to a person and He who made person-hood is the source of what love means.

Do you remember the words of George Frideric Handel when he wrote the "Hallelujah Chorus"? Handel composed *Messiah* in an extraordinary span of just twenty-four days. He didn't leave his house during those three weeks. As he came to the text and music of the "Hallelujah Chorus," he said, "Whether I was in the body or out of the body when I wrote it, I know not," and with tears streaming down his face he added, "I did think I did see all heaven before me, and the great God Himself." Interestingly, he died just eight days after he had conducted his final performance of *Messiah,* and as he lay in bed he wished he would die on Good Friday, "in hopes of meeting his good God, his sweet Lord and Savior, on the day of His resurrection." He almost got his wish, for he died on Good Saturday, and as Paul said, "to be absent from the body" is "to be present with the Lord" (2 Corinthians 5:8 KJV). Handel was with his Lord on that Easter morning. We still look ahead to that reunion. He celebrates now in the presence of the One of whom he wrote and sang.

I believe that wonder is fulfilled in the culmination of gratitude, truth, love, and hope. When we recognize in our hearts our gratitude to God, when we live by His truth, and when we enjoy His love, our hope is strengthened till the day we see Him in the purity of our being as we encounter the pure presence of God.

> But purer and higher and greater will be
> Our wonder, our transport, when Jesus we see.[11]

6

When every sense coalesces in the purpose

for which we are created,

we see reality through our Creator's eyes

and our heart sings in harmony

with His voice.

CHAPTER SIX

Forward to the Past

HAVE YOU EVER BEEN on a weight-loss program? Then you know the greatest difficulty and the most frustrating challenge is to keep the weight off after you have lost it. In fact, it would not be surprising to learn that if the pounds lost over the years by an average individual in sporadic efforts to diet were added up, they would more than total that individual's present body weight! Thankfully, the body is still there and all is not "lost"!

Some things in life are harder to maintain than to attain. Wonder is in that category. To change the nuance, many of us are familiar with the conclusion drawn by Jim Elliot: "He is no fool who gives what he cannot keep to gain that which he cannot lose."[1] In the end, life is like a balance sheet of gains and losses. The real battle lies in knowing what we can afford to lose and what we must uncompromisingly hold on to. Jesus said that it profits a person nothing if he or she gains the whole world but loses his or her soul. Simple reason tells us that it is a mindless transaction to gain what is merely temporal and lose what is desirably eternal. In our desire for wonder so much is transacted every day and so much is lost in the process. The only way to configure a plan is to understand the nature of our hungers and clearly differentiate between the fulfillments that are permanent and those that are temporary. That is the only way to keep our goals realistic.

THE PERMANENCE OF CHANGE

Let's step into a flow of thought in Greek philosophy. The issue of the momentary versus the permanent plagued the Greeks as well. Parmenides argued for the permanence of everything—"Whatever is, is," he said. While things may appear to change in form, in substance they are permanent. Just as energy cannot be created or destroyed but is always there in some form, so life has an indestructibility to it. Whatever is, is. That was non-negotiable. Parmenides stood firm in his unchanging sea.

Heraclitus came along and added one word to that dictum— "Whatever is, is *changing.*" You never step into the same river twice, said he, because the river is in constant flux and out of flux. In fact, it is nothing but flux. The only thing that is permanent is change. Parmenides and Heraclitus would have had quite a debate on the words of the song "Old Man River"—"he just keeps rolling along."

But then came Cratylus to throw his thoughts into the mix. He went one better than Heraclitus. He said, "Not only do you not step into the same river twice, you do not even step into the same river *once.*" Why? Because the river is not the only thing that's changing; you are changing as well. The same you is not constantly you. With the passing of each fraction of a second, your physical and mental makeup is imperceptibly in transition. It is not just that Old Man River keeps rolling along; it is that everything keeps rolling along— man and river in a permanently changing mix. If Yogi Berra didn't say it, he ought to have: "Even nostalgia is not what it used to be."

Humor aside, resolving the dilemma raised by these three thinkers is the starting point of retaining the wonder. How we understand what is permanent and what is changing gives us the answer. But rather than go the route of a rigorous academic exercise, let us approach it where the emotions meet this reality and discover the strength of change in the hands of an unchanging God.

G. K. Chesterton once said that man is a misshapen monster with his feet set forward and his head set back. In other words, he wants to move forward, striving, grasping, climbing, but deep inside he knows that if he is to find rest at the end of the day, he must head back home or he will be dining with a different family each night— and even a banquet gets monotonous if you feast every night. Coming home to where the wonder is, is the way to retain it in perpetual rest of heart. In other words, progress and common points of return are not mutually exclusive ideas. Because origination and destination are identical venues does not expel progress.

You recall the discussion in a previous chapter where I said that Shakespeare was partly onto something when he identified our different stages of life. However, he was mistaken in thinking that advancing one stage meant abandoning the previous one. That is not what God intended. Trying to find permanence in the progressive stages leads us forward and backward, going forth and returning, gaining the right things and losing what must be lost, journeying to our home with head and feet in synchronized motion. Yes, the toy, the balloon, and the rattle widen the young child's eyes. They are entertaining for the very reason that they are new. However, for the same reason that a child cannot differentiate between an electric toy and electricity, he does not know that while the grip of a toy may excite him, the clasp of a live wire will incinerate him. The child simply does not know the dangers. The capacity to enjoy is unlimited, but the capacity to differentiate is highly limited. It is clearly the immaturity of *knowledge*.

There is a similar danger when the child becomes a young adult. Emotions suddenly are expressed by new surges of desire. Boundless energy entices us into boundaryless experiences, while we forget that experimentation has its entailments. We think we can separate ideas from consequences. The truth is that emotions can also be incinerated. New exploits are attempted but the immaturity here is one of *wisdom*.

When the middle years come, new experiences are not in gains and surprises but in the sudden realization of losses. There are very few new things left to experience, along with the haunting awareness of diminishing strength. A deep conflict emerges. The old no longer enchants, but it is the old that stirs the emotion. The head is turned backward, but the feet are moving forward. This is when the heart waffles between hungering for wonder and surrendering any belief that it is even a possibility. This immaturity is one of *discipline,* or perhaps better put, of *balancing the hungers.* Habits have become encrusted and change is resisted. But it is in this very period that the question of permanence and change is faced head-on. Time does bequeath wisdom, and a small window of opportunity remains.

Do you remember C. S. Lewis's powerful book *The Screwtape Letters?* The story line is that a senior devil is instructing a junior devil on how to trip up those who seek to follow the "Enemy," God. The senior devil tells the junior imp, "Work on their horror of the Same Old Thing. The horror of the Same Old Thing is one of the most valuable passions we have produced in the human heart."[2] Middle age is "horrified" by the fact that everything is now the same old thing, and yet it suspects that it is in the old that something of hope is possible.

I have told this story many times but it bears repeating. When our son, Nathan, was about three years old, he was playing with a helium balloon in our living room. He would let it go, watch it rise to the ceiling, climb up on the sofa, grab the string, and pull it down. This was heavenly, and he did it again and again and again. G. K. Chesterton said something to the effect that God's infinite capacity is microcosmically revealed in a child's capacity to exult in the monotonous. Do it again! Do it again! Do it again!

But alas, even repetition for a child has a limit. Nathan decided in favor of variety. He went outside and let the balloon go. All of a sudden he realized that it was not stopping and that there was no sofa to climb on. His wails of despair brought me outside and then he suddenly paused to say, "I know what, Daddy. The next time you are in an airplane, you can get it back for me!" Wonder was still optimistic, but the reality was changing. Some things can be lost. I was his only hope to get it back.

THE OLDER WE GET

THE MORE WE NEED

SOMEBODY BIGGER THAN WE ARE

TO RESTORE WHAT WE HAVE LOST.

In the midst of change and transformation, we realize that the older we get the more we need somebody bigger than we are to restore what we have lost. In *Prince Caspian* C. S. Lewis gives us a magnificent illustration of this. Lucy has just come face to face with Aslan:

> "Welcome, Child," he said.
> "Aslan," said Lucy, "you're bigger."
> "That is because you are older, little one," answered he.
> "Not because you are?"
> "I am not. But every year you grow, you will find me bigger."[3]

God has promised that when we find Him, it is not that everything around us has changed but that we have become new. The old way of looking at things is gone. Retaining while moving forward becomes the glimpse given to the new creation. It is not that there are no more disappointments but that we look at them differently. It is not that there are no more temptations but that we respond to them differently. It is not that there is no more of the same old thing but that we have learned to appreciate and treasure the old things. It is not that nothing is ever lost but that we don't hold on to things in the same way. It is not that nothing is ever new but that we receive it with a different perspective. The more we mature in our thinking the bigger God looks to us, because it is we who need to grow, not He. But how do we move forward and still head home? How do we grow older and still retain the wonder? He has taught us how.

Looking at Looking

It is very interesting to me what God has done to leave His presence with us. If it had been left to us, we would have asked for the constancy of the miracle or the physical presence of His Son. Peter asked for that after the Transfiguration experience. "Can we not just stay here?" he asked. Jesus walked on this earth two thousand years ago; why could He not walk among us now, as well?

Though we may never actually utter those words, we often feel their truth. The flash felt in the moment of conversion. The dramatic answer to a prayer. With the poet we cry, "Where is the joy that once I knew when first I saw the Lord?" Why the monotony now?

Yet when He left His disciples Jesus told them that He would give them something more certain than the miracle or the spectacular. He would give them the "more sure word of prophecy" (2 Peter 1:19 KJV). The Holy Spirit would bring to mind all that they had heard and seen and would inspire them to put it in writing. John's Gospel begins with, "In the beginning was the Word." He ends his writings by saying, "Jesus did many other things as well. If every one of them were written down, I suppose that even the whole world would not have room for the books that would be written" (John 21:25). What is he getting at? Without doubt, to him the supremacy of the word was self-evident. Words. Books. Writing. Those are the seeds of the blessed imagination.

Let's go back to Cratylus for a moment. So radical was his belief about the absoluteness of change that he concluded that one ought not to say anything about anything because at all times both the "sayer" and the "thing" were changing. One ought only to "wag a finger." But he himself said something about the "unsayability" of everything. His theory of reality was unreal because he could not say it and affirm it at the same time.

God knows better and He spoke to us about it. Think of the place words have played in human history. In America's collective memory there may be no more important words than the 272 words uttered by Abraham Lincoln at Gettysburg. But why are words so important?

Think back upon the time you first fell in love. What was it that so stirred your heart when you talked on the telephone or received those love letters? It was a line or a statement, a thought or a promise. At first the words were subtle and their meaning was pondered in hope and expectation. Gradually, the intimations became more overt and there was less doubt about their meaning. Finally, there was a confidence that said, "I know." You did not need 272 words to communicate what you wanted to say or hear; just three words said it all: "I love you." The power of words to stir the heart is the way we human beings relate in hope and trust. From this reality, there are two grand truths that stir the imagination.

The first is that we know there is a difference between looking at something and looking through something. The poet Ruskin said somewhere that a cat may look at a king but a cat cannot see a king. He meant, of course, that a cat cannot appreciate the insignia of royalty. She has no power to discern the symbolism of crown and scepter. A dog's eyes are sharper than our eyes. But place a masterpiece of poetry in front of a dog and it is nothing more than paper with black blotches on it, something to tear up. The dog simply looks *at* the object; he cannot look *through* it.

A few weeks ago, my wife spent considerable time and effort preparing a collage of our children's pictures to present to each of them on Valentine's Day. The last thing she and I did the night before was to look at those pictures and marvel at the memories. Of course, they were beautiful. The next morning, I came downstairs to let our two puppies out for their customary outdoor jaunt. To my utter dismay, I saw that the pictures had fallen from the counter and the two little canines had done an absolutely thorough job of shredding them to pulp. My face was in my hands as they jumped up and down to welcome me, lavishing all their affection on me, completely oblivious to the treasure they had destroyed. They couldn't even see through a *picture,* let alone appreciate any written *words.*

F. W. Boreham reminded us of this great truth in an essay he called "The Telescope." One can look at the geometric design of the telescope and admire its burnished brass rings or its highly polished lenses. But to really admire a telescope you need to pick it up, set it up on a hill somewhere, and then, by placing your sight through the viewing lens, see the starry hosts above and marvel not just at the heavens, but at the incredible telescope that makes such viewing possible.

There is a world of difference between looking at something and looking through something. We make the same colossal mistake with God's Word and the gift of print. We have books all around us. We stack them on our shelves. Yet He has revealed Himself in His Word and we let it lie unstudied, unread, and sometimes untouched. We look *at* it. We hardly ever look *through* it.

In Psalm 119 David set out to enumerate the blessings of God's Word and revelation. The fascinating thing about that 176-verse treatise is that 171 of those verses refer to God's Word, and the whole tribute to the Word is words within words. For rather than just lay out the marvelous power of God's Word, David formatted his psalm in alphabetical order from the *aleph* to the *tav*, or as we would say, from A to Z. God's Word exhausts the very alphabet. There is nothing in the world more important than knowing and understanding how the written Word points beyond language to the very author of speech.

The second thing is that words are more than carriers of thought pointing beyond themselves. They are bridges. Lincoln's words bridged the past to the present and into the future. The words "I love you" do the same—shaped by the past, glorying in the present, hoping for the future. Words are bridges between people and time. God's Word is the best bridge between the old and the new, between the body and the soul, between the temporal and the eternal, between God and humanity. The inscription is old but the blessing is always new. The language is old but the application is new. The originals are old but the originality is new—the forward and the backward.

Let me illustrate this for you. Not long ago, I was speaking at the University of Michigan. Through the courtesy of some friends I was invited to visit what is considered the largest papyrus collection in the Western Hemisphere. Papyrus was the writing material in the ancient world, and the word is actually the very origin of the English word *paper.* But papyrus itself refers to a plant, native to the swamps of Egypt and Sudan and to the textured sheets made from the stem of that plant. The collection at the university ranges from 1000 B.C. to A.D. 1000. The archivist showing us these treasures treated them with the utmost respect and care. These rolls and fragments were preserved within the dry sands of Egypt beneath the ruins of ancient cities. The sand, which is infestation-free, preserved the documents for thousands of years. Now, the collection is housed in a room with precise controls for temperature and humidity as air is circulated through special filters to keep the papyri from pollutants and particles that could destroy it. There are barriers in the room that prevent water and fire penetration. Alarm systems provide warning of any unauthorized entry or breakdown in environmental controls. Any slight alteration of temperature puts the material at risk. Therefore, even entering that narrow corridor where the papyri are stored is highly restricted.

The archivist was able to take us into the vault merely for a minute or two and then brought out the "treasures" just a few at a time, locking the door each time. He showed us a little boy or girl's homework from two thousand years ago—it included some alphabet exercises in Greek and yes, some doodling, too. The original was old, but to this very day children still do their homework and doodle at the same time. There was a letter from a young Egyptian lad writing from Rome to his mother in Egypt and telling her months after his departure that he had arrived safely in Rome and was now enlisted in the Roman navy. He didn't know how often she would hear from him but if he heard of anyone heading to Egypt he would make sure to send a letter with that person. The limitations of mailing and letter writing are now old, but the longing of a mother's heart to hear from her son is still new.

One by one we saw these precious documents, sandwiched in glass. Just touching the glass was a thrill. But then the archivist said, "Now for the best, which I have saved for the last," and he displayed parts of the Chester Beattie collection that included several of Paul's writings to the Romans, Corinthians, Ephesians, and other New Testament epistles. We just stood there overwhelmed with this nearly two-thousand-year-old piece of papyrus. Among the collection was the twenty-sixth chapter of the Gospel of Matthew. My colleague and I bent over and read it carefully. Yes, in a somewhat smudged Greek text but incredibly clear for its age, we were able to read the portions of Matthew's Gospel that included the story of the woman with the alabaster ointment, the warning to Peter that he would deny his Lord, the betrayal of Judas, the commemoration of Holy Communion, and the heart-wrenching prayer Jesus prayed at Gethsemane. There was a hushed silence in the room as we read it, and as we finished, my colleague, forgetting for the moment that I was still recovering from major back surgery, slapped me a hard hurrah on my back. All I could do was swallow the pain while devouring the soul-sustaining bread of life before me.

I felt the same jubilation. This is God's Word. It is eternally true. It is needed for instruction, for reproof, for righteousness, and yes, for the freshness of His voice every morning. Whoever copied the words of the original manuscript onto those papyri little dreamed that God would preserve it with its timeless truths over so much time. The text before us recorded Jesus' words to the woman with the alabaster ointment, telling her that what she had done in worship of the Lord would be told wherever the gospel was preached. And here, in a room in the University of Michigan two thousand years later, we saw, touched, and reveled in Christ our eternal contemporary. We mistakenly demean the trans-temporal nature of God's Word when we think of it as the "same old thing." It is the timeless new thing like fresh dew on parched grass, like water to a thirsty soul, and thirst is never only a thing of the past.

I should add something here. It is indisputable that there is nothing in the ancient classics like the Bible, with such extraordinary textual support in the large number of texts so close to the original. But this was the treasure—old texts with truth as new to our hearts today as it was for the writers so long ago.

GOD'S WORD

IS THE DEPOSIT MADE

IN THE MEMORY BANK

OF THE SOUL.

There are times in all of our lives when the only thing that will see us through a tough spot is God's Word. In the film *Chariots of Fire,* there is a gripping event that takes place minutes before the Scottish runner Eric Liddell is about to run the race of his life. That part of the film is exactly the way it actually happened. Eric Liddell had taken a difficult stand in his bid to win the gold medal in the 1924 Olympics in Paris. He had trained hard for the 200 meters, but just days before the event, he found out that the heats were to be held on a Sunday. It was against Liddell's conviction to run on the Lord's day. So he told his coach he was pulling out of the event.

The entire coaching staff and the management tried to talk him out of it and even considered dropping him altogether. They finally decided that if they were successful in persuading him to set aside his deep convictions, it would change who he was and affect how he ran. So they let him run in the 400-meter race, an event that was not his primary strength.

The moment came and he was on the track for the race. Just before they took to their marks, Jackson Schulz, the American runner, walked over to Eric and handed him a piece of paper. On it were written the words from 1 Samuel 2:30 (KJV): "'Them that honour me I will honour,' says the Lord." Eric Liddell clutched that piece of paper and ran the race of his life, winning the gold. He looked beyond the words to the author of His conviction and he clung to the truth that showed what true winning is all about.

David said it best: "I have hidden your word in my heart that I might not sin against you" (Psalm 119:11). Until we learn to treasure that Word and look through it to the source of all life, we too will be like little puppies ripping into the imagination and leaving it in tatters. God's Word is the deposit made in the memory bank of the soul. That is the bank that provides the capital from which to draw when life exacts a cost. Living off that capital provides the wonder in perpetuity, for heaven and earth may pass away but His Word abides forever. We may change, but His Word does not change because it is true for every stage of life, in every circumstance. It keeps us in touch with the new. It keeps us real in our expectations, promising not a trouble-free trip but God's presence in every trial. It keeps our feet in tune with our head and provides strength for the journey, all the way.

READING ABOUT READING

But there is more to reading than the Word alone. There is the very discipline of reading and, I might add, *what* we read. I am a writer and I have some deep struggles in the Christian faith. It is not with my faith, but with the way I see it abused and, if you will, treated as something trite and shallow by those who claim to be believers. There are books by the score on the shelves of Christian bookstores. Check them out. What do they point to? Is it to the nobler and higher and richer truths of God, or is it to more of ourselves? Thankfully the nobler and higher truths are there, but for the most part, judging by the titles and content, one would think the Christian faith is all about me and how I feel and what I want. There are books on happiness by the score, how to succeed in a variety of ways. Stop. Ponder. Reason. Is your own reading shallow or deep? The wonder that you will find in the shallow end can only be for a child. Swimming in the deep is for the mature. If a follower of Jesus does not mature in his or her reading, the church could end up running the biggest nursery in the world.

Some time ago, my wife and I were visiting the ancient monasteries of Meteora in Greece, situated above the country town of Kalabaka in western Thessaly. These edifices are precariously perched upon surreal configurations of spindly rock upon rock, resembling meteors or spiraling stalagmites suspended in midair. The sight is breathtaking. In these monasteries the monks are devoted to studying just the "sacred text." Anything outside of the Scriptures is considered to be deadly to the soul. So seriously did the authorities of bygone years take that narrow view that the pages of any other book, such as the writings of Aristotle, etc., were dusted with a thin coating of arsenic. This way, when a monk secretly daring to read from these books moistened his finger to turn the page, he would by the moment be unknowingly poisoning himself until he would suddenly drop dead. The poor monks did not know why one by one their mates were dying, but the "Grand Inquisitors" knew that punishment had been meted out for those "cheating" on their reading.

Today, I cannot help but wonder if the lunacy of such beliefs and methods is outdone by the mindlessness of some of the stuff we ingest in our reading. What poison do we take in by our reading that leads us to false expectations in the Christian life, thereby manufacturing false wonder and denying us the real thing?

When the apostle Paul was in prison he wrote to his spiritual son, Timothy, asking for his cloak and his books. How often have we read or heard that it was the books or thoughts from their reading that helped a person in dire straits in prison or in a situation of danger to survive and triumph through the situation? G. K. Chesterton was once asked for the one thing he would want if he were stranded on an island with no hope of any outside rescue. His answer was as practical as his wit: "Why, a book on boat building, of course!" If wonder is to be retained in our mind, reading and reading *well* is indispensable to the imagination and the heart. Good reading is like looking for something you have lost and finding it, but in the search finding something else that had also been lost. That is how wonder is constantly replenished.

THINKING IS A

DYING DISCIPLINE

IN A SOCIETY

THAT THROBS WITH ACTIVITY.

THINKING ABOUT THOUGHT

If reading is the first component of retaining wonder, reflection is the second. I have often been asked as I have carried out my responsibilities and calling over the years how one remains fresh in one's thinking and able to keep one's heart sensitive to the newness of God's touch. I know of no better answer than to be in regular times of solitude and quietness before our Lord. In our harried and hurried lifestyles we work and rush and meet and talk. We take very little time to think. Thinking is a dying discipline in a society that throbs with activity.

A few years ago I was reading *The Return of the Prodigal Son* by Henri Nouwen. He begins the book by describing an experience that completely changed his life. Nouwen was a professor at Harvard University and struggled with whether he was in the right place of his calling. On a trip to St. Petersburg, Russia, he visited the Hermitage Museum in order to see one particular painting, Rembrandt's portrayal of the prodigal son. In that painting, Rembrandt captures the moment when the son is returning home and the father is rushing out to meet him.

Nouwen described his emotions as he studied the painting, not for ten minutes or even for an hour. He sat before that painting for several hours. He pored over every stroke of color, every wrinkle on the father's skin, every hint of unmitigated delight at the sight of his son, every mark on the son's downtrodden but hopeful face, every ray of sunlight in the painting as real as if it beamed through the canvas. After uninterrupted hours of concentration, he got up a changed man. He returned home, resigned his position at Harvard, and until his sudden and seemingly untimely death, worked at a home for the mentally retarded in Toronto, Canada. This great writer of devotional themes devoted his life to loving those who were in such special need. Unhurried reflection on a piece of art changed scores of lives.

There is tragedy in my telling that story. You see, I have been to the Hermitage Museum as well. But I do not remember even seeing that painting. Why? We were in a rush to pay a hurried visit and then leave. Over the years, I now wonder what blessings I have robbed myself of in life for not pausing to think.

I know a fine woman who told me an incredible story about her life. Her marriage was breaking up when she became pregnant in a forced episode. Angry and distraught, she decided to abort the baby. She told nobody else that she was pregnant but drove herself to an abortion clinic, her heart already set. She paid in cash for the procedure up front and was in the procedure room waiting for the doctor to arrive. As he was about to inject her with the needle and begin the process of abortion, the door swung open and the nurse said he had an urgent call that he had to take. "I'll be back in a moment," he said, as he put down the syringe and left the room.

Alone for these few moments, she happened to turn around and caught sight of the monitor on which the sonogram was showing the little one in her womb. Immediately, she was stricken by the gravity of what she was doing. With fresh courage, she dressed and walked out of the clinic without even pausing to pick up the money and left with her heart in turmoil at what she had almost done.

Today that infant in the womb is a young girl on the verge of womanhood. She is her mother's closest friend and is completely unaware of how close she came to being eliminated. When I thanked the mother for her courage to make the right decision, she said, "No, it was not me. There was another voice within me that said this was the right thing to do. It was of God."

But this is what our society is so afraid to do in our day, is it not: to pause, to think, to reflect, to listen? I shudder to think of all that has been aborted in life, of creative ideas and so much else that has been lost to the imagination when we do not even think of the decisions we make or of the deeds we practice.

Into this rushing lifestyle have come theories on meditation

WONDER

IS RETAINED BY

WISE PONDERING.

telling us how to think on nothing until we realize we are divine inside. The Scriptures do not tell us to empty our minds and think nothing but to exercise the minds God has given us to think on things that are true, noble, right, pure, lovely, admirable, excellent, or praiseworthy (see Philippians 4:8), to meditate on His law (see Psalm 119:97), and "to take captive every thought to make it obedient to Christ" (2 Corinthians 10:5). So little of this is done that the mind becomes incapable of living in silence for even a short span of time. Wonder is retained by wise pondering. Unless we learn to think and reflect on things above we will reflect the hollowness of a world moving fast but slow to think.

I believe it was to give us opportunity to reflect that God instituted festivals. In the life of the Hebrew nation these festivals were periods of the year set apart to focus on a different aspect of their spiritual journey with God. To those who had come after the Exodus, the seasons and their respective celebrations were carved into their calendars. In the spring they were to celebrate Passover as they remembered God's saving grace. In the summer they were to respond as a blessed community at the Feast of Pentecost. In the autumn they were to renew their commitments at the Feast of Tabernacles. With the season came the reminder to think of the great truths of God's work in their midst. Let us consider just one of these festivals to stir our hearts with wonder.

To the ancient Hebrew, Passover was the time to think of the Exodus and the provision of the lamb that was offered for their redemption from Egypt. Now as the redeemed community, we, the church universal, look back at the offering of our Lord on Good Friday. I would like to think that we take the time to think on these things.

A student at a university said to me, "I often wonder about Jesus struggling at Gethsemane over the impending crucifixion. What was happening there? Jesus asking to be spared the cup? It sounds crazy to me," he said.

I answered, "Ponder with me for a moment. The cup of human sin was to be drunk to the last dregs by the purest one of all. The most painful physical torture was that of being crucified. Yet the Lord Jesus did not fear the physical pain. The only indivisible entity in the world is the very Holy Trinity. The possibility of His Father turning away from Him when He was subjected to the accursedness of sin was paramount in His mind. But He knew that if that was the only way to accomplish salvation, He would do it.

"Think further. There are realities in the human experience that cannot be mitigated until they have been seen for what they are. Evil and love are two such truths. There is nothing so horrific as evil and yet we have tried to deny its existence. The Hindu calls it Maya—nonreal, illusionary, having a different context in appearance than in actuality. The Muslim denies original sin. The Buddhist believes you can work your way through the maze of reincarnations till all evil, that is, *desire,* is shaken off and we are left desiring nothing.

"Look at the Cross, now. Evil is seen for what it is—all the vileness in the human heart is there in the face of the perfectly pure. Evil is not covered up. See again the marvel of God's love that offers forgiveness of such evil. But even as forgiveness is offered, evil and love are seen in their full force in the triumph of one over the other. Only in the Christian faith will you see the reality of evil and love concretely expressed even as forgiveness and hope are made possible by the sure grace of God."

There was silence and then the student said one word: "Awesome." He muttered again, "Just awesome."

How can we not think about these things? The hymn writer says:

> I sometimes think about the Cross,
> and shut my eyes, and try to see
> The cruel nails and crown of thorns,
> and Jesus crucified for me.
>
> But even could I see Him die,
> I could but see a little part
> Of that great love, which, like a fire,
> is always burning in His heart.[4]

Days come and go, Good Fridays come and go, and we have not pondered the mystery of evil and the majesty of love. Somewhere in the silence within a voice beckons, but the sounds of activity block us from entering that sobering place. Over the last few years I have

> WONDER ENRICHES YOU WHEN YOU
>
> TAKE THE TIME TO REFLECT AND TO
>
> PONDER THE GREATNESS OF
>
> OUR FAITH IN JESUS CHRIST.
>
>

made it a practice to rise early and go down to a room alone. I pace the floor, I kneel, I read . . . only to listen. For you see, at the end of the day if you have spoken but not listened, you have spent without income and sooner or later an expenditure of words without an income of ideas will lead to conceptual bankruptcy. Wonder enriches you when you take the time to reflect and to ponder the greatness of our faith in Jesus Christ.

TALKING ABOUT TALK

The third necessary way to retain wonder is to delight in discussion. But it is not the discussion that one has in groups where the goal is to keep the discussion at the rudimentary level for the seeker. That is good and has its place. But there are scores for whom the rudimentary level is the only level they ever reach and the mind is never challenged to go deeper and reach higher. I think with envy of the discussions around a table that the likes of C. S. Lewis and J. R. R. Tolkien had with others. How they must have sharpened each other with their wit and their wisdom. How they plumbed thoughts that spawned their own works. I delight in the company of those who enrich my thinking.

F. W. Boreham said, "It puts iron into the blood to spend time with one for whom the claim of conscience is supreme and who loves the truth of God with so deathless an affection." What a thought! How beautifully put! How true! In fact, Boreham himself relayed numerous conversations he had with one named John Broadbanks. His readers did not know until his latter years that there was no such person. It was a person he made up to give himself an alter ego with whom to think aloud and sharpen his own thoughts. We all need a "Broadbanks" in our lives, but how wonderful it would be to have a real person like that and not just an imaginary one.

I think of a walk in the Bible that I would love to have taken—that walk along the Emmaus road when Jesus opened the Scriptures to two disciples walking with Him. After their discussion with Jesus, the disciples said, "Were not our hearts burning within us while he talked with us on the road and opened the Scriptures to us?" (Luke 24:32). There was the ultimate bridge of the past, the present, and the future. That is the kind of discussion I mean—where you plan time with those who think well, who think deeply, and who think about things that really matter. This is not an accountability group, as important as that is. This is a group of people committed to deepening their walk with Christ and who are disciplined in study and interaction.

I walked one day with Malcolm Muggeridge, that great English journalist, when he was in his latter years. He took me into his private room of memorabilia where displayed on the walls were pictures of great men and women, noted heads of state and others he had interviewed. Those three hours moved at the speed of light, but they are hours I will remember forever. Every minute was like a bite of infinity, loaded with nourishment for the soul. Education cannot give you that kind of thinking. I believe that if the church is to survive the onslaught of a world barren of thought it will have to be a place where thinking is restored.

There is a magnificent psalm that was sung at weddings in its time. The psalm begins with the words, "My heart is stirred by a noble theme ... my tongue is the pen of a skillful writer ... in behalf of truth, humility and righteousness" (Psalm 45:1, 4). The heart gripped by a theme, the pen gripped by skill, and all in behalf of truth and righteousness—that is our shaping and our calling.

Aldous Huxley once remarked of our frivolous culture, "It is no longer a question of a Good Time coming; for The Good Times have gone with the arrival of A Good Time All The Time." Much of the talk we hear around us is on an ignoble theme. Even humor seems to be funny anymore only if it is vulgar. The reason is that humorists have lost the heart of nobility and the skill that is in tune with the heart. So they descend to that which shocks and draws a reaction. The time will come when even the vulgar doesn't shock anymore. Only noble themes lift the spirits to heights of grandeur and the heights of the mind can never be exhausted. Wherever two or three are gathered, noble themes can enrich them and prepare them for the hazards in life.

In *The Incendiary Fellowship,* Quaker philosopher Elton Trueblood said, "Though I am as conscious as are most people of the inadequacies of the local church and though I am sure that the church is not the building . . . I can never forget that, apart from the poor little fellowships in such poor buildings, there isn't a chance in the world that I would be enlisted in the cause of Christ."[5]

That is the church—a place simple in its appearance but profound in its talk.

> IN THE CLOSET
>
> OF OUR LIVES
>
> LIES THE FULLNESS OF
>
> HIS RICHES.
>
> ⸎

A PRAYER ABOUT PRAYER

I do not believe that wonder can ever be retained apart from learning the discipline and delight of prayer. In the closet of our lives lies the fullness of His riches. In the secret place lie unmined treasures. Prayer is at once the place of victory and yet the place into which we are so reticent to step. So much has been said about prayer over the years that it almost seems predictable. But let me just state two profound reminders. If those are grasped the sudden light of its beauty will dawn.

The early church father John Chrysostom said this of prayer:

The potency of prayer hath subdued the strength of fire, it hath bridled the rage of lions, hushed anarchy to rest; extinguished wars, appeased the elements, expelled demons, burst the chains of death, expanded the gates of heaven, assuaged diseases, repelled frauds, rescued cities from destruction, stayed the sun in its course, and arrested the progress of the thunderbolt. Prayer is an all-sufficient panoply, a treasure undiminished, a mine which is never exhausted, a sky unobscured by the clouds, a heaven unruffled by the storm. It is the root, the fountain, the mother of a thousand blessings.[6]

We can either dismiss this as mere rhetoric or face the grim fact that prayerlessness is the scavenger of wonder. If prayer is indeed the root, the fountain, and the mother of a thousand blessings, then prayerlessness is the seed and weed of the destruction of a thousand blessings. It is here that we win or lose.

But it is also here that we face the greatest challenge. The discipline of praying is the seedbed of retaining wonder. For here God brings our wills into alignment with His, enabling us to face both the grim and the triumphant and put them in the context of the greater story. Prayer is not the means of bringing our wills to pass but the means by which He brings our will into line to gladly receive His will. And what a glad moment that is. Find a plan for your time of prayer and implement it to His honor and glory and your joy and sustenance.

Robert Browning once wrote:

> When I see boys ride a-cockhorse,
> I find it in my heart to embarrass them

By hinting that their stick's a mock horse,
And they really carry what they say carries them.[7]

My deduction is that a praying Christian is carried by wonder; a "prayerless" person carries the wonder and will soon get exhausted by carrying the infinite.

THE WONDER OF WORSHIP

As we look back upon the journey we have traveled, this is what we conclude. The components of gratitude and truth, love and hope bring the realization of wonder. The disciplines of study, of reading and reflecting, of dialoguing in depth and praying with belief sustain the wonder. In short, wonder is captured in one word—worship. When we have learned what worship is, we have experienced what wonder is. Worship is a personal thing before it goes public. It is an individual thing before it is part of a community. It is a disciplined thing before it is natural.

In that sense, worship is not only a science in that there is discipline to it, but worship is an art in that there is beauty to it. For here the emotion, propelled by the will, touches deep into the imagination to lift the spirit into the very presence of God. On our journey to the home of our Father, He has given us the map and shown us what it will cost. There is a language to it, there are boundaries for it, and there is danger in it. The recognition that though some days will be hard and painful and other days will be joyous and delightful, all are part of the same journey. We must keep our eye on Him and the delight of reunion with Him, bearing the good with the hard and accepting all as real, but letting none diminish the grand, ultimate sight and sound of His presence. If we are to sing in the company of those who have found wonder through worship, we must be girded by the sword of His Word, be guided by the great ones who have walked this way before, and be patient in knowing that the journey is long and will not be accomplished in a day. But if the feet and the head are facing in the same direction, the emotions will follow as well.

God is like the light. Wonder is like the shadow. If you chase the shadow you will never catch up to it. It might even disappear. If you walk toward the light, the shadow will always pursue you. That is when the heart sings with gladness.

> Surely goodness and mercy will follow me
> all the days, all the days of my life.[8]

I have often wished I could sing with a great voice that would resonate in the grandest halls of this world or in every open space where listeners of truth would want to hear of the beauty and power of His wonder. If I could have a voice like that, there is one song I could sing. It would be:

> Fairest Lord Jesus, Ruler of all nature,
> O Thou of God and Man the Son;
> Thee will I cherish, Thee will I honor
> Thou my soul's glory, joy, and crown.

> Fair are the meadows, fairer still the woodlands,
> Robed in the blooming garb of spring;

Jesus is fairer, Jesus is purer,
Who makes the woeful heart to sing.

Fair is the sunshine, fairer still the moonlight,
And fair the twinkling starry host;
Jesus shines brighter, Jesus shines purer,
Than all the angels heaven can boast.

All fairest beauty, Heavenly and earthly,
Wondrously, Jesus, is found in thee;
None can be nearer, fairer or dearer,
Than Thou my Savior art to me.[9]

He is the one who lifts my sights and my heart through the wonders that are all around to the greatest wonder of all—Himself.

Keep your sights on Him. Spread the wonder. Become part of a community that knows what this means and nurtures it with truth. You will both recapture and retain the wonder.

ENDNOTES

CHAPTER ONE:
WE MISS IT, BUT WHAT IS IT?

1. Arthur Sullivan and Adelaide Proctor, "The Lost Chord," 1877.
2. Henry Sloan Coffin, *Communion through Preaching* (New York: Charles Scribner's Sons Ltd., 1952), 16–17.
3. Quoted in Chet Raymo, *Skeptics and True Believers: The Exhilarating Connection between Science and Religion* (New York: Walker and Company, 1998), 20.
4. Thomas Carlyle, *Sartor Resartus: The Life and Opinions of Herr Teufelsdrockh,* available at http://cupid.ecom.unimelb.edu.au/het/carlyle/sartor.html.
5. Miguel De Unamuno, *Tragic Sense of Life,* trans. J. Crawford Flitch (Mineola, N.Y.: Dover Publications, 1990).
6. Used by permission.

ENDNOTES

CHAPTER TWO:
THE RULES OF THE GAME

1. Greg Asimakoupoulos, "Longing for the Days of Childhood," in *Prayers from My Pencil: Personal Psalms for Everyday Believers* (Wheaton, Ill.: Mainstay Church Resources, 2001).
2. William Shakespeare, *As You Like It,* Act II, Scene 7.
3. William Shakespeare, *Macbeth,* Act V, Scene 5.
4. Neil Postman, *The Disappearance of Childhood* (New York: Vintage Books, 1994), 81.
5. Blaise Pascal, *Mind on Fire* (Portland, Ore.: Multnomah, 1989), 55.
6. Paraphrased from G. K. Chesterton, *Orthodoxy* (reprint, Nashville: Thomas Nelson, 2000), 213.
7. Christopher Morley, "No Coaching," from Halford E. Luccock and Frances Brentano, eds., *The Questing Spirit* (New York: Coward-McCann, Inc., 1947), 418.
8. "The Wonder of It All," George Beverly Shea. Copyright © 1956, 1957 by Chancel Music. Assigned 1985 Word Music, Inc. (a division of Word Music Group, Inc.).

CHAPTER THREE:
PASSIONATE PURSUIT, MISDIRECTED SEARCH

1. John Howard Griffin, *Black Like Me* (New York: Signet, 1960), 15–16, quoted in Leonard Griffith, *Take Hold of the Treasure: Life in the Christian Faith* (Toronto: The Anglican Book Centre, 1980), 103.
2. Ravi Zacharias, *Sense and Sensuality: Jesus Talks with Oscar Wilde* (Sisters, Ore.: Multnomah, 2002).
3. Oscar Wilde, *De Profundis.*
4. For more information about Haing Nor's life, refer to the following: http://news.bbc.co.uk/1/hi/world/americas/79289.stm.

5. "A Hundred Years of Thinking About God," *U.S. News & World Report,* 23 February 1998.

CHAPTER FOUR:
WONDER UNWRAPPED

1. Bernard of Clairvaux, "O Sacred Head, Now Wounded," 1153, trans. Paul Gerhardt.
2. Edwin Arlington Robinson, "Captain Craig," 1902.
3. A. B. Simpson, "Himself."
4. Quoted in *The Jerusalem Post International Edition,* 8 February, 1997, 4.
5. Quoted in Anthony Cave Brown, *Bodyguard of Lies: The Extraordinary True Story Behind D-Day* (New York: HarperCollins, 2002), 10.
6. Philip Novak, *The Vision of Nietzsche,* Jacob Needleman, gen. ed. (London: Element Books, 1996), 10–11.
7. Ibid.
8. Alfred Lord Tennyson, "In Memoriam A.H.H.," 1833.
9. From "Truth and God," a lecture by Mahatma Gandhi, delivered 31 December 1931 in Lausanne, Switzerland. For further information go to http://meadev.nic.in/Gandhi1/truth&god.htm.
10. Malcom Muggeridge, *The Green Stick* (Glasgow: William Collins and Sons, 1972), 19.
11. James Russell Lowell, "The Present Crisis," 1844.

CHAPTER FIVE:
WONDER CONSUMMATED

1. John Donne, "A Hymn to God the Father," in *The Oxford Book of English Verse, 1250–1900* (New York: Oxford University Press, 1926), 230.

2. Quoted in Leonard Griffith, *Take Hold of the Treasure: Life in the Christian Faith* (Toronto: The Anglican Book Centre, 1980), 102.

3. George Matheson, "O Love That Wilt Not Let Me Go," 1882.

4. J. H. Oldham, *Life Is Commitment* (London: S. C. S. Press, Ltd., 1953), 24.

5. I am indebted to Bishop Lightfoot for this insight.

6. William Cowper, "On the Receipt of My Mother's Picture," 1798.

7. William Cowper, "God Moves in a Mysterious Way," 1779.

8. F. W. Boreham, *A Bunch of Everlastings* (London: Epworth Press, 1940), 113.

9. Elizabeth Barrett Browning, *Aurora Leigh,* book 7, lines 821–24.

10. C. S. Lewis, *Weight of Glory* (Grand Rapids, Mich.: Eerdmans, 1979), 4.

11. Fanny Crosby, "To God Be the Glory," 1875.

CHAPTER SIX:
RETAINING THE WONDER

1. Quoted in Elisabeth Elliot, *In the Shadow of the Almighty* (New York: Harper & Row, 1958), 108.

2. C. S. Lewis, *The Screwtape Letters,* rev. ed. (New York: Collier, 1982), 116.

3. C. S. Lewis, *Prince Caspian,* chapter 10.

4. William Walsham How, "It Is a Thing Most Wonderful," 1872.

5. Quoted in Leonard Griffith, *Take Hold of the Treasure* (Toronto, Canada: The Anglican Book Centre, 1980), 37.

6. Quoted in Leonard Ravenhill, *Why Revival Tarries* (Minneapolis: Bethany Fellowship, 1959), 156.

7. Robert Browning, "Christmas Eve," 1850.

8. John W. Peterson, "Surely Goodness and Mercy."

9. Author unknown, "Fairest Lord Jesus" (emphasis added).